Gettin
for the Ne
Testing Program

ughton
fflin
rcourt

Grade 4

GO MATH!

Blackline Masters

INCLUDES:

- Prerequisite Skills Inventory
- Beginning-of-Year, Middle-of-Year, and End-of-Year Benchmark Tests
- Chapter Tests
- All Assessments in the Format of the New York State Testing Program
- Individual Record Forms
- Correlation to Standards

Printed in the U.S.A.

ISBN 978-0-544-85027-9

4 5 6 7 8 9 10 1186 25 24 23 22 21 20 19 18 17 16

4500632409 B C D E F G

Contents

Tests and Management Forms

Overview of *GO Math!* Assessment

How Assessment Can Help Individualize Instruction

The *Getting Ready for the New York State Testing Program* contains several types of assessment for use throughout the school year. The following pages will explain how these assessments can be utilized to diagnose students' understanding of the New York State Mathematics Learning Standards and to guide instructional choices, improve students' performance, and help facilitate students' mastery of this year's objectives.

Diagnostic Assessment

Prerequisite Skills Inventory in the *Getting Ready for the New York State Testing Program* should be given at the beginning of the year or when a new student arrives. This short-answer test yields insight regarding understanding of prerequisite skills. Test results provide information about the review or intervention that students may need in order to be successful in the coming year. Suggestions for intervention are provided for this inventory.

Beginning-of-Year Test in the *Getting Ready for the New York State Testing Program* is a mixed-response-format test comprised of multiple-choice, short-answer, and extended constructed-response items. This test should be utilized early in the year to establish on-grade-level skills that students may already understand. This benchmark test will allow customization of instructional content to optimize the time spent teaching specific objectives. Suggestions for intervention are provided for this test.

Formative Assessment

Middle-of-Year Test in the *Getting Ready for the New York State Testing Program* assesses the same skills as the Beginning-of-Year Test, allowing monitoring of students' progress to permit instructional adjustments when required.

Summative Assessment

Chapter Test in the *Getting Ready for the New York State Testing Program* measures students' mastery of concepts and skills taught in the chapter. The test assesses the mastery of the New York State Mathematics Learning Standards taught in the chapter. It is a mixed-response-format test comprised of multiple-choice, short-answer, and extended constructed-response items.

Performance Tasks in the *Getting Ready for the New York State Testing Program* provide assessment of each grade level's Critical Areas. Each task assesses the students' ability to use what they have learned and provides an opportunity for students to display their thinking strategies. Correlations to the New York State Mathematics Learning Standards and performance indicators are provided. Use the associated rubric to score these assessments.

End-of-Year Test in the *Getting Ready for the New York State Testing Program* documents each student's level of mastery of the concepts and skills for the current grade level and mirrors the Beginning- and Middle-of-Year Tests. Used together, these mixed-response-format tests allow for monitoring of growth throughout the year.

New York State Testing Program Assessment Formats

The New York State Testing Program consists of assessments that contain mixed responses comprised of multiple-choice, short-answer, and extended constructed-response items. This allows for a more robust assessment of students' understanding of concepts. The New York State assessment is administered via several "books" and *GO Math!* presents items in formats similar to what students will see on the tests. The following information is provided to help teachers familiarize students with these different types of items. An example of each item type appears on the following pages. You may want to use the examples to introduce the item types to students. The following explanations are provided to guide students in answering the questions.

Example 1 Divide a two-digit number by a one-digit number.

Multiple Choice

For this type of item, students respond to a single question with several choices. There are directions similar to, "How many objects are in each group?" Students must circle the correct letter to make their choice. There will only be one choice that is correct.

Example 2 Add fractions.

Short Answer

This type of item will ask students to solve a problem and show their work. The students will need to explain how they got their answers. They may need to make or complete a drawing to show their work. Tell the students to think about their answers carefully. There are some questions that will have more than one correct answer.

Example 3 Solve and explain a problem with multiple parts.

Extended Constructed Response

This type of item will ask students to solve a problem that has two parts. The students will be expected to show their work. This can be shown with an explanation or with a drawing. Tell them to think about their answers carefully. There are some questions that will have more than one correct answer.

Example 1

A class of 35 students is divided into 5 equal groups for a class project. How many students are in each group?

A 5

B 6

C 7

D 8

Example 2

Martha and Dan are raking leaves in a yard. So far Martha has raked $\frac{1}{10}$ of the leaves, and Dan has raked $\frac{8}{100}$ of the leaves. What fraction of the leaves have they raked together?

Show your work

Answer ____ of the leaves

Example 3

To rent a delivery van, it costs $1.75 per mile, plus the cost of gas at $0.50 per mile. There is also a fixed cost of $40. The expression $1.75n + 0.50n + 40$ gives the total cost, in dollars, for renting the van and driving n miles.

PART A

What is another way to write the expression? Explain.

Answer ______________________________

____

____

____

PART B

How much would it cost to rent the van and drive it for 8 miles?

Show your work

Answer __________

Name ______________________________

Write the correct answer.

1. The ice skating rink rented 238 pairs of ice skates one weekend. What is 238 rounded to the nearest hundred?

____

2. The theater has 329 fixed seats and 174 moveable seats. What could be a **reasonable estimate** of the total number of seats in the theater?

____

3. On Saturday, the lifeguard counted 416 swimmers at the beach. On Sunday the lifeguard counted 283 swimmers at the beach. How many swimmers were at the beach in all?

____

4. Mr. Li drove 287 miles from Hawk City to Bear Town. He then drove 175 miles from Bear Town to Cedar City. How many miles did Mr. Li drive in all?

____

5. Hector earned 942 points in his first round of a video game. Sarah earned 791 points in her first round of the same video game. What could be a **reasonable estimate** of how many more points Hector earned than Sarah in the first round of the video game?

____

6. Mrs. Rourke's class collected 385 cans during a recycling drive. Mr. Hardy's class collected 259 cans during the same recycling drive. How many more cans did Mrs. Rourke's class collect than Mr. Hardy's class?

____

GO ON

7. Campers go to Ridgeline Camp for one week sessions. During the first week of camp, there were 112 campers. During the second week, there were 15 fewer campers than in the first week. How many campers were at camp during both weeks?

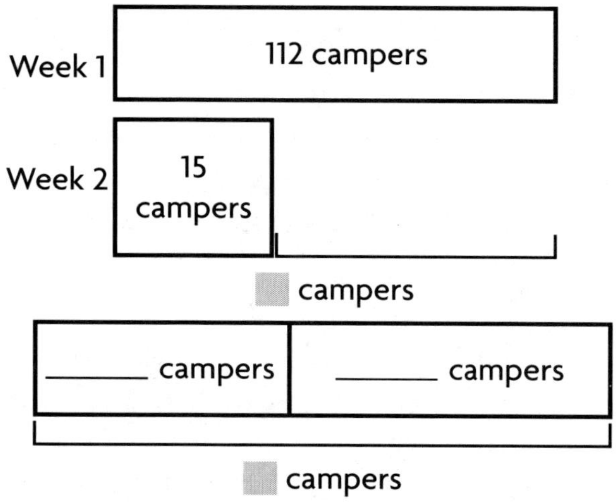

____

8. A seamstress measured the lengths of several ribbons. She recorded the data in the line plot below.

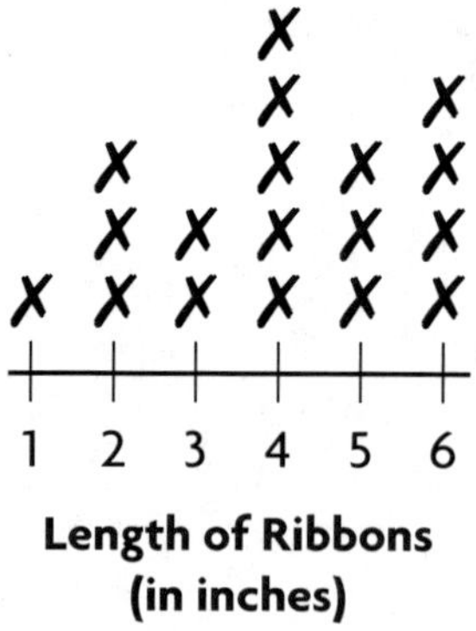

How many ribbons are 5 inches long?

____

9. Kevin divided his model airplane collection into 3 groups. Each group has 5 airplanes.

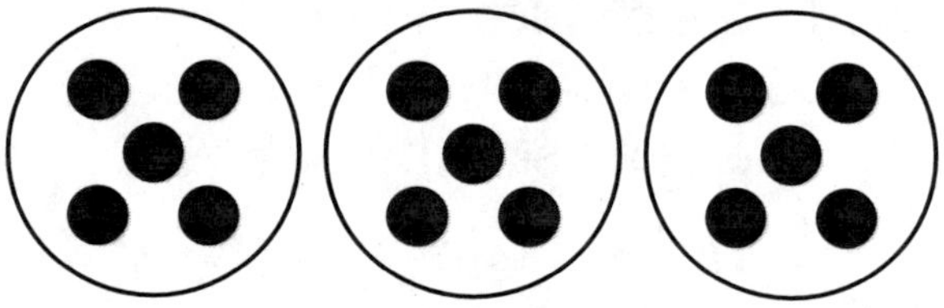

How many model airplanes does Kevin have in his collection?

____

10. There are 4 jars for markers in Maya's class. Maya found 0 markers in each jar. Write a number sentence that shows how many markers Maya found in all.

____

____

11. Mrs. Murphy bought 2 boxes of granola bars. Each box has 6 bars. How many granola bars did Mrs. Murphy buy in all?

____

GO ON

12. Wendy writes a pattern of numbers.

21, 28, 35, 42, 49

How can you describe this pattern?

____

13. Find the pattern used in the table. Then complete the table.

Necklaces	2	3	4	5	6
Beads	18	27	36		

____

14. Sam plans to buy 24 slices of pizza for a party. There are 8 slices in each whole pizza. How many pizzas does Sam need to buy?

$$p \times 8 = 24$$

____

15. One pack of construction paper has 40 sheets of paper. How many sheets are in 6 packs?

____

16. Omar writes a set of related facts. One of the facts he writes is $30 \div 5 = 6$. Write an equation that is included in the same set of related facts.

____

____

17. Melody brought 5 bones to the dog park. She gave an equal number of bones to each of 5 dogs. How many bones did Melody give to each dog?

____

18. Simone wants to put 10 photos on each page of her scrap book. She has picked out 70 photos she wants to use. How many scrap book pages does Simone use?

____

19. A school lunch table seats 6 students. How many lunch tables are needed to seat 18 students?

____

GO ON

20. Brad's little brother has a storage box for his toy cars. Each section of the box holds 8 toy cars. How many sections does the box have if it holds 56 cars?

____

21. Ryan arranged 40 blocks in 8 equal rows. How many blocks are in each row?

____

22. Susie separates 18 stickers into 9 equal groups. How many stickers are in each group?

____

23. Luke needs to divide a sheet of paper into two equal parts. Draw a line to divide the square into 2 equal parts.

24. Toni made a model to show the number of students on the playground. The shaded part of the model shows the fraction of students on the slide.

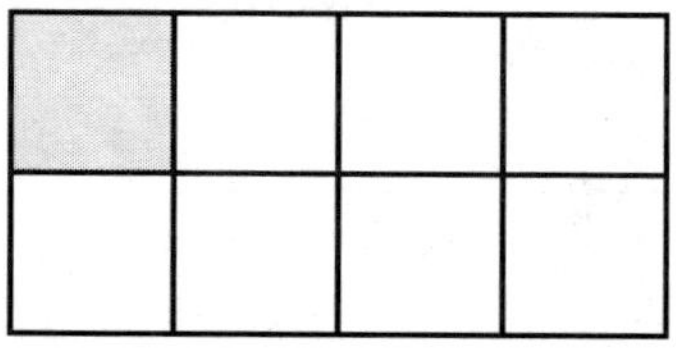

What fraction of students are on the slide?

____

25. A student shaded this model. The shaded part shows what part of the pottery glazes in the art room have glitter in them.

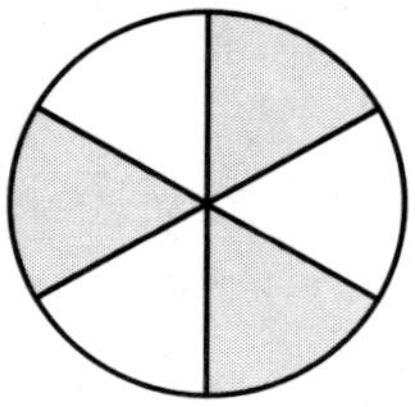

What fraction of the pottery glazes have glitter?

____

26. Mrs. Parker bought $\frac{3}{4}$ pound of strawberries and $\frac{1}{4}$ pound of raspberries. Write a statement to compare the amounts of berries.

____

____

GO ON

27. Of all the students in Matea's class, $\frac{2}{3}$ are wearing sneakers and $\frac{2}{6}$ are wearing sandals. What symbol compares the fractions correctly? Write $<$, $>$, or $=$.

$$\frac{2}{3} \bigcirc \frac{2}{6}$$

28. A scientist measures the lengths of three beetles. The first beetle is $\frac{4}{8}$ inch long. The second beetle is $\frac{2}{8}$ inch long. The third beetle is $\frac{7}{8}$ inch long. Write the fractions in order from **least** to **greatest**.

____

29. Hannah is selling slices of pie at the bake sale. The pie has 8 slices. She has sold $\frac{1}{4}$ of the slices.

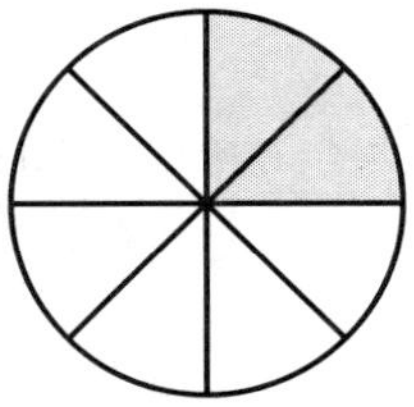

What fraction with a denominator of 8 is equal to $\frac{1}{4}$?

____

30. Jake looked at the clock before leaving for school. The hour hand was between the 7 and the 8. The minute hand was on the 9. What time did Jake leave for school?

____

31. Ling started running at 10:18 A.M. She finished running at 10:50 A.M. How long did Ling run?

____

32. A batch of muffins needs to bake in the oven for 24 minutes. Scott puts the muffins in the oven at 2:17 P.M. What time will he take the muffins out of the oven?

____

33. Latonya fills a drinking glass with water. Write *more than 1 liter*, *about 1 liter*, or *less than 1 liter* to estimate how much water the glass will hold.

____

GO ON

34. Julia wants to find the mass of her backpack filled with books. Write *grams* or *kilograms* to name the **best** unit to use to find the mass of the filled backpack.

____

35. Jillian uses a balance to compare the masses of the objects shown. Use the words *is less than, is the same*, or *is more than* to compare the masses of the objects.

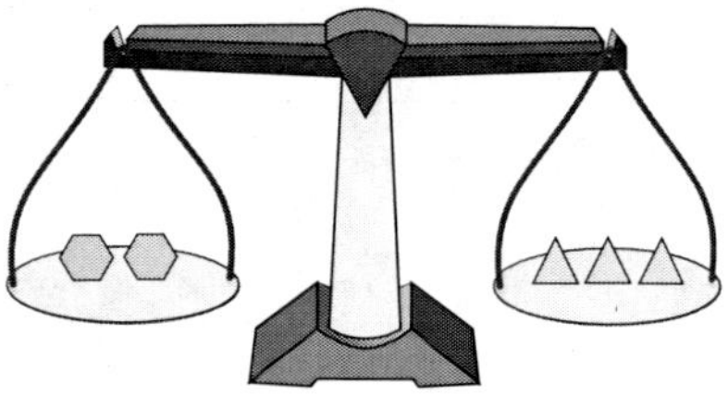

____

36. How many right angles does this shape appear to have?

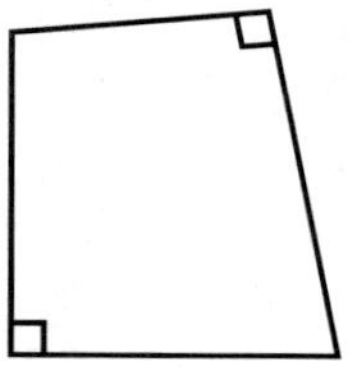

____

37. Carrie drew this shape. Use *right angle, less than a right angle*, or *greater than a right angle* to describe the marked angle.

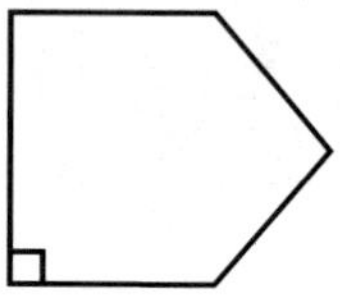

____

38. Hank used line segments to draw a shape. Look at the bold sides of his shape.

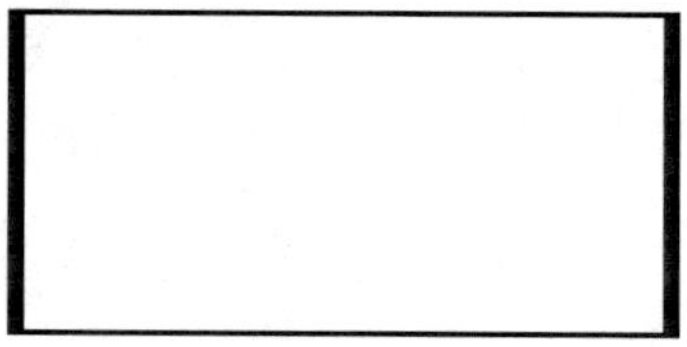

Write *intersecting, perpendicular*, or *parallel* to describe the sides.

____

39. Blake drew this shape.

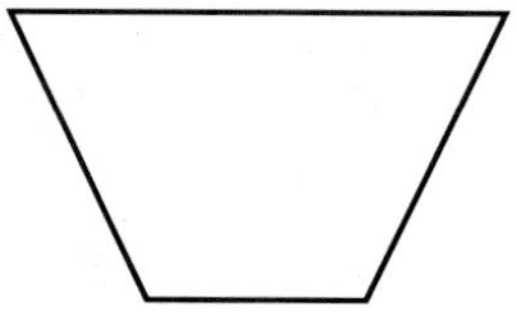

Name Blake's quadrilateral.

____

40. Lisa drew a quadrilateral with 4 right angles. The parallel sides are equal length. Which quadrilateral did she draw?

____

STOP

Name ______________________________

Choose the correct answer.

1. Daniel plans to use a strategy to find 18×470. Which expression shows a strategy he could use?

A $18 \times 0 \times 470$

B $4 \times 5 \times 470$

C $3 \times 6 \times 470$

D $6 \times 3 \times 47$

2. Michelle manages a function hall. She purchases 415 napkins each week for the first two weeks of June. Michelle purchases 550 napkins each week for the first three weeks of July. Her supplier forgot to send 67 napkins. How many napkins did Michelle receive those 5 weeks?

A 898

B 2,413

C 2,480

D 2,547

3. A factory can make 2,035 markers in one hour. Which is the **best** estimate of how many markers can be made in 6 hours?

A 1,200 markers

B 2,000 markers

C 12,000 markers

D 20,000 markers

4. Multiply 7×72. Which of the following statements is true?

A The product is 490.

B A reasonable estimate of the product is 490.

C Using partial products, the products are 140 and 49.

D Using regrouping, 14 ones are regrouped as 4 tens and 1 one.

5. Matthew walks $\frac{8}{10}$ mile to Zach's house. Which fraction in hundredths is equal to $\frac{8}{10}$?

A $\frac{8}{100}$

B $\frac{80}{1000}$

C $\frac{80}{100}$

D $\frac{800}{100}$

GO ON

6. Anna jogged $1\frac{3}{10}$ miles on a path in the park. What is this distance written as a decimal?

A 0.13 mile

B 1.03 miles

C 1.3 miles

D 13 miles

7. Rico walked for $\frac{3}{10}$ mile. Then he walked for $\frac{24}{100}$ mile. How far did he walk in all?

A $\frac{54}{100}$ mile

B $\frac{5}{10}$ mile

C $\frac{30}{100}$ mile

D $\frac{27}{100}$ mile

8. What is the measure of the unknown angle in the figure?

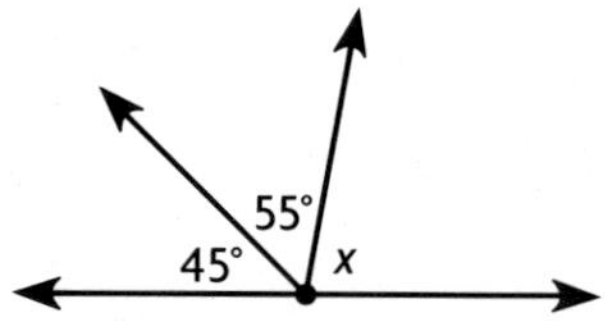

A 180°

B 100°

C 80°

D 70°

9. David drew the angle below.

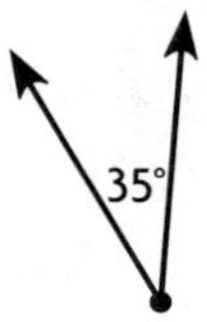

What name should David give his angle?

A obtuse angle

B acute angle

C right angle

D straight angle

10. Maria put two angles together to form a straight angle. One angle measures 112°. What is the measure of the other angle?

A 78°

B 68°

C 58°

D 48°

GO ON

Name ________________________________

11. A circle is divided into parts. Which sum could represent the angle measures that make up the circle?

A $120° + 160°$

B $110° + 120° + 130°$

C $90° + 100° + 110° + 120°$

D $60° + 60° + 60° + 60° + 60°$

12. Flora needs $\frac{3}{8}$ yard of blue ribbon and $\frac{2}{8}$ yard of red ribbon to make a bow for a present she is wrapping. How much ribbon does Flora need in all?

A $\frac{1}{8}$ yard

B $\frac{5}{16}$ yard

C $\frac{5}{8}$ yard

D $\frac{7}{8}$ yard

13. Which of the following shows the Associative Property?

A $\frac{3}{5} + \left(\frac{2}{5} + \frac{1}{5}\right) = \left(\frac{3}{5} + \frac{2}{5}\right) + \frac{1}{5}$

B $\left(4\frac{1}{8} + \frac{1}{8}\right) + 2\frac{7}{8} = 4\frac{1}{8} + 2\frac{7}{8} + \frac{1}{8}$

C $3\frac{1}{5} + \left(5 + 1\frac{3}{5}\right) = 3\frac{1}{5} + \left(1\frac{3}{5} + 5\right)$

D $\left(\frac{4}{10} + \frac{1}{10}\right) + \frac{6}{10} = \left(\frac{4}{10} + \frac{1}{10}\right) + \frac{6}{10}$

14. Mark rode his bike $\frac{22}{8}$ miles. Which mixed number shows the fraction of miles he rode his bike?

A $2\frac{6}{8}$ miles

B $2\frac{4}{8}$ miles

C $2\frac{3}{8}$ miles

D $2\frac{1}{8}$ miles

15. Mark had $4\frac{1}{4}$ bottles of water for his track meet. When he finished the meet, he had $1\frac{3}{4}$ bottles of water left. How many bottles of water did Mark use?

A $2\frac{2}{4}$

B $3\frac{1}{4}$

C $4\frac{1}{4}$

D 5

GO ON

16. Kayla has 36 flower stickers, 27 bird stickers, and 18 butterfly stickers. She wants to put an equal number of stickers into bags so all of the bags will be the same. How many of each kind of sticker can Kayla put in each bag?

A 9

B 1 or 9

C 1, 3, or 9

D 1, 3, 9, 12, or 18

17. Leah and Tony were playing a game. Leah was counting by 8s. Tony was counting by 3s. They paced the counting so they would say the first common number together. What is the first number they both said together?

A 12

B 24

C 32

D 36

18. Chen's friend Bob is helping him learn about prime numbers. Bob writes a list of numbers and asks Chen to choose the prime number. Which number should Chen choose?

A 12

B 24

C 31

D 36

19. Liz and Dave made a secret code. They wrote some numbers in the code to help them remember the pattern.

8, 11, 10, 13, 12, 15, 14, 17

What should be the next number in the code?

A 15

B 16

C 18

D 20

20. The Simmons family is taking a 2-week vacation to Alaska. How many days will their vacation last?

A 7 days

B 14 days

C 21 days

D 24 days

GO ON

21. The table shows a pattern for two units of customary length.

______	______
1	12
2	24
3	36
4	48

Which are the best labels for each column?

A Miles, Yards

B Yards, Feet

C Yards, Inches

D Feet, Inches

22. The tour of the space museum started at 10:45 A.M. It lasted for 1 hour 30 minutes. What time did the tour end?

A 11:15 A.M.

B 11:45 P.M.

C 12:15 P.M.

D 1:15 P.M.

23. Patrick mixed 3 quarts 1 pint of orange juice with 3 pints of cranberry juice and 1 pint of grape juice to make punch. How much punch does he have?

A 5 quarts 1 pint

B 5 quarts

C 4 quarts 1 pint

D 4 quarts

24. Karen scored 157,834 points on the third level of her computer game. What is the value of the digit 5 in 157,834?

A 500,000

B 50,000

C 5,000

D 500

25. Maria used number tiles to make the number 538,397. Jimmy used number tiles to make the number 583,397. Which statement about these numbers is correct?

A $583,397 < 538,397$

B $583,397 > 538,397$

C $583,397 = 538,397$

D $538,397 > 583,397$

GO ON

26. Pete's Pizza sold 65,182 pizzas the first year they were open. They sold 58,458 pizzas the second year. What was the total number of pizzas sold during the first two years of business?

A 113,640

B 123,540

C 123,630

D 123,640

27. A total of 539,838 visitors went to a theme park during June and July. If 322,741 visitors went to the theme park in June, how many visitors went to the theme park in July?

A 217,097

B 217,197

C 539,838

D 862,579

28. Roberta used 90 centimeters of ribbon to make a border around a rectangular card. The length of the card is 20 centimeters. How many centimeters is the width of the card?

A 15

B 20

C 25

D 70

29. Which of the following could be the dimensions of a rectangle with a perimeter of 70 inches?

A length: 15 inches; width: 15 inches

B length: 20 inches; width: 15 inches

C length: 30 inches; width: 10 inches

D length: 35 inches; width: 5 inches

30. Mr. Wilson is building a new patio off the back of his house.

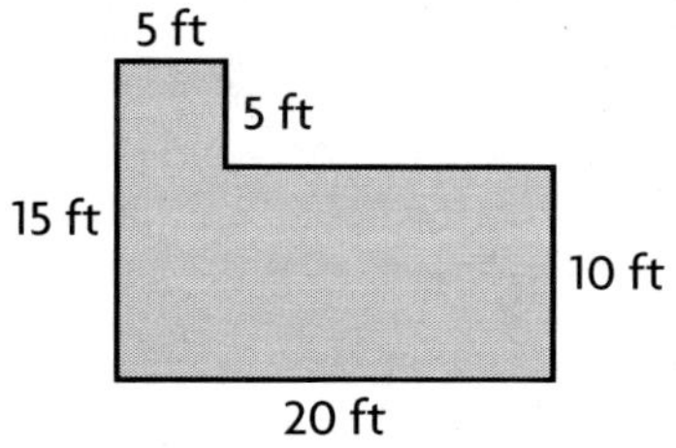

How much tile does Mr. Wilson need to cover his patio?

A 60 square feet

B 200 square feet

C 225 square feet

D 275 square feet

GO ON

31. One wall of Eric's bedroom is 15 feet wide and 8 feet high. A door on the wall is 7 feet high and 3 feet wide. How much wall paper will Eric need to cover the wall?

A 120 square feet

B 110 square feet

C 99 square feet

D 89 square feet

32. Which shows the **best** estimate to use to find 43×28?

A $40 \times 20 = 800$

B $45 \times 25 = 1{,}125$

C $40 \times 30 = 1{,}200$

D $50 \times 30 = 1{,}500$

33. Sofia can text 40 words in one minute. At that rate, how many words can she text in 12 minutes?

A 400

B 480

C 580

D 720

34. A pizza restaurant's customers bought 85 pizzas at $18 each. What is the total amount customers paid for the pizzas?

A $1,430

B $1,490

C $1,530

D $1,620

35. The Best Read bookstore has 48 boxes of books to be unpacked. Each box contains 24 books. How many books in all need to be unpacked?

A 1,052

B 1,125

C 1,132

D 1,152

GO ON

36. Yoshi says he needs a board that is $\frac{17}{4}$ feet long. How can Yoshi rename the fraction as a mixed number?

A $5\frac{1}{4}$

B $4\frac{1}{4}$

C $3\frac{1}{4}$

D $2\frac{1}{4}$

37. Marsha named a fraction that was **not** a multiple of $\frac{3}{6}$. Which fraction could she have named?

A $\frac{6}{6}$

B $\frac{9}{6}$

C $\frac{11}{6}$

D $\frac{15}{6}$

38. Carlos lives $\frac{3}{8}$ mile from his school. He walks to school each morning and gets a ride home after school. How far does Carlos walk to school in 5 days?

A 1 mile

B $1\frac{3}{4}$ miles

C $1\frac{7}{8}$ miles

D $2\frac{7}{8}$ miles

39. Khloe used $2\frac{1}{4}$ gallons of paint on her living room walls. She used 4 times as much paint for her kitchen and dining room walls. How many gallons of paint did Khloe use for the kitchen and dining room walls?

A 9

B 8

C $6\frac{1}{4}$

D $4\frac{2}{4}$

40. Cassandra and her four sisters divided 1,068 stickers equally. About how many stickers did each girl receive?

A 100

B 150

C 200

D 250

GO ON

Name ___________________________

41. Steven needs 42 stickers to decorate a poster he is making. The stickers come on sheets of 12. How many sheets of stickers should Steven buy?

A 5

B 4

C 3

D 2

42. A store gave away 1,498 calendars in 7 days. They gave away the same number of calendars each day. How many calendars did the store give away each day?

A 21

B 204

C 214

D 224

43. A cookie factory packs 6 small cookies in a sample pack. The factory gives the sample packs to visitors. How many sample packs can they make with 1,800 cookies?

A 3,000

B 300

C 30

D 3

44. Jared drew the figure below.

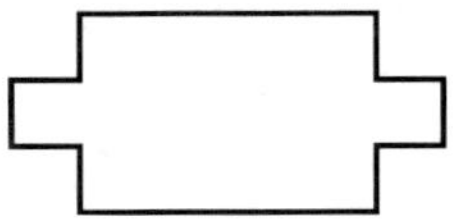

How many lines of symmetry does the figure have?

A 4

B 3

C 2

D 1

45. Bella drew the figure below as an example for her classmate.

Which of the following terms **best** describes the figure Bella drew?

A line segment

B line

C angle

D ray

GO ON

46. Brianne has a sticker that looks like a quadrilateral that has only 1 pair of parallel sides, 1 pair of equal sides, and no right angles. Which figure could be the shape of Brianne's sticker?

A 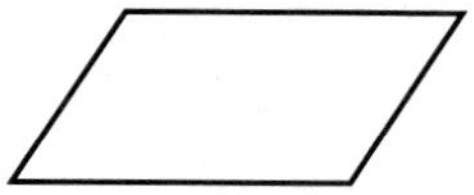

B 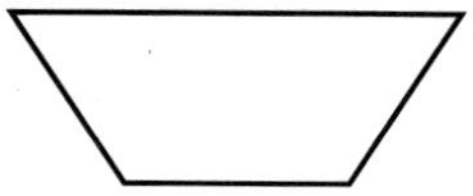

C 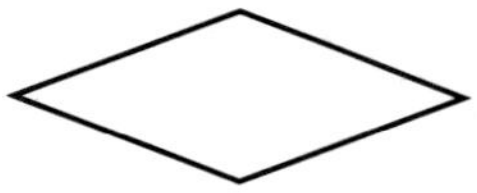

D 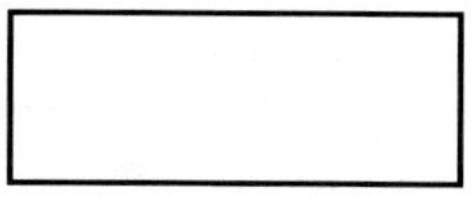

47. A sign is in the shape of an obtuse triangle. Which of the following could be the shape of the sign?

A 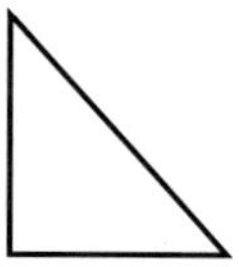

B 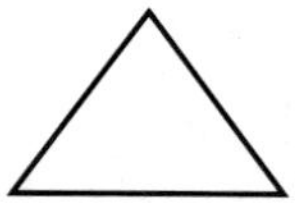

C 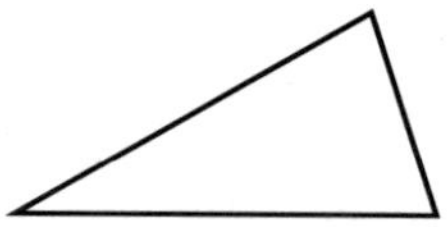

D 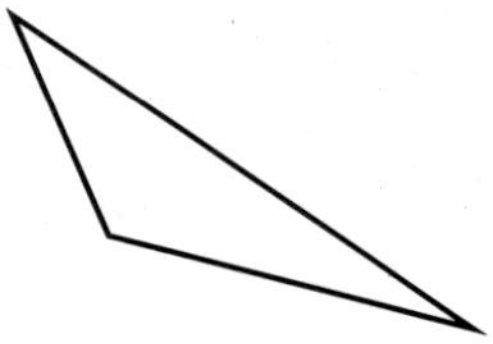

48. Luisa ran $\frac{3}{5}$ mile yesterday and $\frac{1}{2}$ mile today. Which number is a common denominator for $\frac{3}{5}$ and $\frac{1}{2}$?

A 12

B 10

C 5

D 2

49. Blake fills an aquarium $\frac{5}{7}$ full of water. Which fraction is equivalent to $\frac{5}{7}$?

A $\frac{4}{6}$

B $\frac{25}{49}$

C $\frac{10}{14}$

D $\frac{10}{7}$

50. Jasmine cut $\frac{3}{8}$ yard of blue ribbon and $\frac{1}{3}$ yard of red ribbon to decorate a package. Which statement correctly compares the fractions?

A $\frac{1}{3} > \frac{3}{8}$

B $\frac{1}{3} = \frac{3}{8}$

C $\frac{3}{8} > \frac{1}{3}$

D $\frac{3}{8} < \frac{1}{3}$

GO ON

Name ________________________________

51. Edward is finding the product of 22 and 31. Edward's answer is incorrect. What did Edward do wrong? What is the correct product?

$$\begin{array}{r} 22 \\ \times\ \ 31 \\ \hline 220 \\ +\ 660 \\ \hline 880 \end{array}$$

Answer ________________________________

____

____

52. Amanda began her math homework at 6:00 P.M. She stopped at 6:45 P.M. How many degrees did the minute hand move while Amanda was doing homework? Explain how you found your answer.

Answer ________________________________

____

____

____

GO ON

53. Samantha and two of her friends have three quarters, one dime, and one nickel to spend. If Samantha and her friends share the money equally, how much will each person get?

Show your work.

Answer ____

54. Michael works in a toy store that sells bags of blocks. He puts 10 blocks in each bag, and $\frac{7}{10}$ of the blocks are red.

PART A

If Michael makes 4 bags of blocks, how many red blocks does he need? Explain your answer.

Answer ____________________

____

____

PART B

Yesterday Michael used 42 red blocks to fill bags. How many blocks that are not red did he use to fill the bags? Explain your reasoning.

Answer

____

____

____

____

STOP

Name ______________________

Choose the correct answer.

1. John plans to use a strategy to find 32×120. Which expression shows a strategy he could use?

A $4 \times 8 \times 12$

B $4 \times 8 \times 120$

C $8 \times 4 \times 100$

D $32 \times 0 \times 120$

2. Natalia manages a function hall. She rented 367 silverware sets each week for the the first three weeks of October. She also rented 410 silverware sets each week for the first two weeks of November. The rental company forgot to send 54 silverware sets. How many silverware sets did Natalia receive those five weeks?

A 777

B 1,867

C 1,964

D 1,975

3. A factory can produce 3,120 cars in a week. Which is the **best** estimate of how many cars the factory can produce in 4 weeks?

A 1,200

B 2,000

C 12,000

D 20,000

4. Multiply 6×57. Which of the following statements is true?

A The product is 366.

B A reasonable estimate of the product is 360.

C Using partial products, the products are 420 and 30.

D Using regrouping, 42 ones are regrouped as 2 tens and 4 ones.

5. Brenda walks $\frac{9}{10}$ mile to the park to meet Daphne. Which fraction in hundredths is equal to $\frac{9}{10}$?

A $\frac{90}{1,000}$

B $\frac{900}{1,000}$

C $\frac{90}{100}$

D $\frac{900}{100}$

GO ON

6. Jack jogged $2\frac{5}{10}$ miles on a path in the park. What is this distance written as a decimal?

A 0.25 mile

B 2.5 miles

C 5.2 miles

D 25 miles

7. Roberto walked for $\frac{6}{10}$ miles. Then he walked for $\frac{25}{100}$ miles. How far did he walk in all?

A $\frac{31}{100}$ mile

B $\frac{35}{100}$ mile

C $\frac{85}{100}$ mile

D $\frac{95}{100}$ mile

8. What is the measure of the unknown angle in the figure?

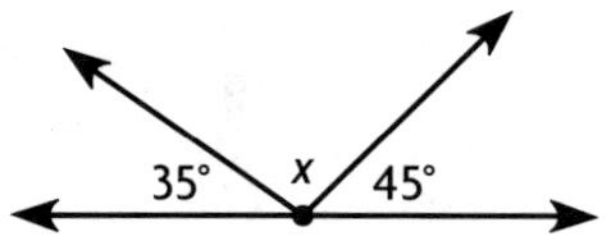

A 180°

B 100°

C 90°

D 80°

9. Melanie drew the angle below.

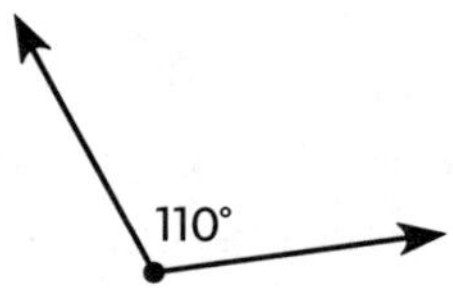

What name should Melanie give her angle?

A obtuse angle

B acute angle

C right angle

D straight angle

10. Miko put two angles together to form a straight angle. One angle measures 88°. What is the measure of the other angle?

A 92°

B 82°

C 72°

D 42°

GO ON

11. A circle is divided into parts. Which sum could represent the central angle measures that make up the circle?

A $180° + 80°$

B $120° + 110° + 30°$

C $160° + 140° + 90° + 70°$

D $72° + 72° + 72° + 72° + 72°$

12. Rosa needs $\frac{5}{12}$ yard of blue ribbon and $\frac{6}{12}$ yard of yellow ribbon to trim a banner she is making. How much ribbon does Rosa need in all?

A $\frac{11}{12}$ yard

B $\frac{11}{24}$ yard

C $\frac{3}{4}$ yard

D $\frac{1}{2}$ yard

13. Which of the following shows the Associative Property?

A $\frac{4}{9} + \left(\frac{2}{9} + \frac{1}{9}\right) = \left(\frac{2}{9} + \frac{1}{9}\right) + \frac{4}{9}$

B $\left(\frac{3}{5} + \frac{1}{5}\right) + 2\frac{8}{10} = \left(\frac{1}{5} + \frac{3}{5}\right) + 2\frac{8}{10}$

C $6\frac{1}{6} + \left(4 + 2\frac{5}{6}\right) = 6\frac{1}{6} + \left(2\frac{5}{6} + 4\right)$

D $\left(5\frac{1}{4} + \frac{1}{4}\right) + 3\frac{3}{4} = 5\frac{1}{4} + \left(\frac{1}{4} + 3\frac{3}{4}\right)$

14. Ryan rode his bike $\frac{18}{4}$ miles. Which mixed number shows the fraction of miles he rode his bike?

A $4\frac{3}{4}$ miles

B $4\frac{2}{4}$ miles

C $4\frac{1}{4}$ miles

D $4\frac{1}{8}$ miles

15. Jacob had $5\frac{2}{3}$ bottles of water for his track meet. When he finished, he had $3\frac{1}{3}$ bottles of water left. How many bottles of water did Jacob use?

A $2\frac{1}{3}$

B $2\frac{2}{3}$

C $5\frac{2}{3}$

D 6

GO ON

16. Maya has 28 apples, 12 oranges, and 8 mangos. She wants to put an equal number of each kind of fruit into baskets so all of the baskets will be the same. How many of each kind of fruit can Maya put in each basket?

A 4

B 1, 2 or 4

C 1 or 4

D 1, 3, 4, 6, or 8

17. Molly and Brian are playing a game. Molly is counting by 8s. Brian is counting by 6s. They pace the counting so they will say the first common number together. What is the first number they both say together?

A 12

B 18

C 24

D 32

18. Eric's friend Hiroshi is helping him learn about prime numbers. Hiroshi writes down a list of numbers and asks Eric to choose the prime number. Which number should Eric choose?

A 8

B 11

C 16

D 32

19. Don texts a number pattern to his friend Lou.

4, 8, 6, 10, 8, 12, 10, 14

Lou texts the next number in the pattern back to Don. What is the number?

A 18

B 15

C 12

D 10

20. Mark's family has lived in the same town for 3 years. How many months have they lived in the town?

A 36 months

B 32 months

C 30 months

D 24 months

GO ON

21. The table shows a pattern for two units of customary weight.

______	______
1	16
2	32
3	48
4	64

Which are the **best** labels for each column?

A Yards, Feet

B Kilograms, Grams

C Tons, Pounds

D Pounds, Ounces

22. The bus left for the nature center at 9:15 A.M. The trip there took 1 hour 45 minutes. What time did the bus arrive at the nature center?

A 11:00 A.M.

B 10:45 A.M.

C 10:15 A.M.

D 10:00 A.M.

23. Pedro mixed 1 pound 6 ounces of apples with 1 pound 4 ounces of oranges and 12 ounces of strawberries to make a fruit salad. How much fruit salad does he have?

A 3 pounds 6 ounces

B 3 pounds 4 ounces

C 3 pounds

D 2 pounds 6 ounces

24. Kevin's brother got 738,256 hits on his new website. What is the value of the digit 7 in 738,256?

A 7,000

B 70,000

C 700,000

D 7,000,000

25. Tina used number tiles to make the number 327,869. Jeremy used number tiles to make the number 327,689. Which statement about these numbers is correct?

A $327{,}689 < 327{,}869$

B $327{,}689 > 327{,}869$

C $327{,}689 = 327{,}869$

D $327{,}869 < 327{,}689$

GO ON

26. Paul got a new video game. He scored 35,698 points on his first game and 48,735 points on his second game. What was the total number of points for both games?

A 84,433

B 84,423

C 84,333

D 74,433

27. A total of 628,349 visitors went to a theme park during June and July. If 296,184 visitors went to the theme park in June, how many visitors went to the theme park in July?

A 167,842

B 245,178

C 308,617

D 332,165

28. Melanie used 80 centimeters of ribbon to make a border around a rectangular card. The length of the card is 30 centimeters. How many centimeters is the width of the card?

A 10

B 15

C 20

D 35

29. Which of the following could be the dimensions of a rectangle with a perimeter of 90 inches?

A length: 25 inches; width: 10 inches

B length: 30 inches; width: 15 inches

C length: 40 inches; width: 10 inches

D length: 35 inches; width: 5 inches

30. Mr. Lee drew these plans for a new garden in his backyard.

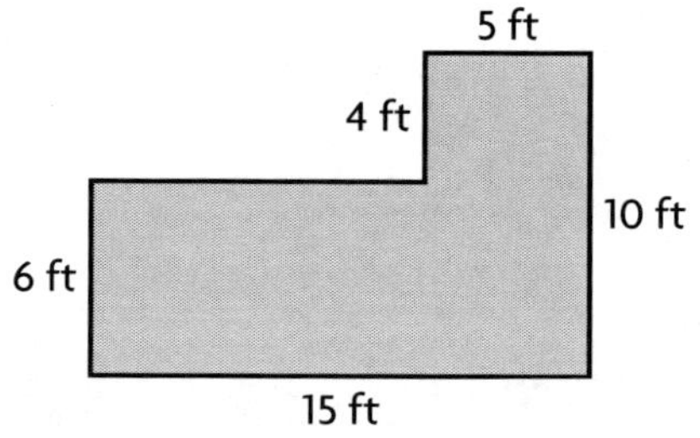

What will the area of Mr. Lee's garden be?

A 150 square feet

B 110 square feet

C 90 square feet

D 40 square feet

GO ON

31. Joseph's notebook cover is 12 inches by 8 inches. He put a wildlife sticker on the notebook. If the sticker is 3 inches by 2 inches. How much of the notebook cover is still showing?

A 108 square inches

B 96 square inches

C 90 square inches

D 84 square inches

32. Which shows the **best** estimate to use to find 18×62?

A $20 \times 70 = 1{,}400$

B $20 \times 60 = 1{,}200$

C $20 \times 50 = 1{,}000$

D $10 \times 70 = 700$

33. Miko can type 70 words in one minute. At that rate, how many words can she type in 12 minutes?

A 800

B 820

C 840

D 880

34. A CD store's customers bought 76 CDs at $16 each. What is the total amount customers paid for the CDs?

A $1,216

B $1,186

C $1,116

D $532

35. Marjorie has 36 boxes of video games to unpack and put on shelves. Each box contains 28 video games. How many video games in all need to be unpacked?

A 2,008

B 1,008

C 968

D 908

GO ON

36. Megan says she needs a piece of rope that is $\frac{15}{6}$ feet long. How can Megan rename the fraction as a mixed number?

A $3\frac{3}{6}$

B $2\frac{3}{6}$

C $2\frac{1}{3}$

D $1\frac{3}{6}$

37. Carla named a fraction that was **not** a multiple of $\frac{3}{8}$. Which fraction could she have named?

A $\frac{6}{8}$

B $\frac{9}{8}$

C $\frac{12}{8}$

D $\frac{14}{8}$

38. Marko runs $\frac{3}{5}$ mile 3 times a week. How far does Marko run each week?

A $3\frac{3}{5}$ miles

B $2\frac{2}{5}$ miles

C $1\frac{4}{5}$ miles

D $1\frac{3}{5}$ miles

39. Jennifer used $3\frac{2}{3}$ gallons of paint on her living room walls. She used 3 times as much paint for her kitchen and dining room walls. How many gallons of paint did Jennifer use for the kitchen and dining room walls?

A 11

B 10

C $7\frac{1}{3}$

D $5\frac{2}{3}$

40. Emily and her four sisters divided 2,039 stickers equally. About how many stickers did each girl receive?

A 200

B 350

C 400

D 550

GO ON

41. Jared needs 54 balloons to decorate a room for a birthday party. The balloons come in packages of 20. How many packages of balloons should Jared buy?

A 5

B 4

C 3

D 2

42. A new pet store handed out 2,472 coupons in 4 days. They handed out the same number of coupons each day. How many coupons did the store hand out each day?

A 61

B 518

C 608

D 618

43. A sock factory packs 5 pairs of socks to a package. How many packages can they pack with 3,000 pairs of socks?

A 6 packages

B 60 packages

C 600 packages

D 6,000 packages

44. Andrew drew the figure below.

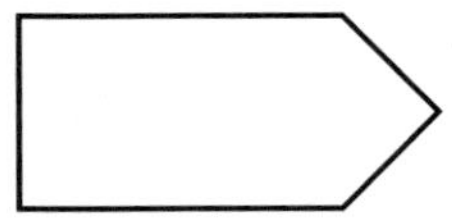

How many lines of symmetry does the figure have?

A 4

B 3

C 2

D 1

45. Julie drew the figure below as an example for her classmate.

Which of the following terms **best** describes the figure Julie drew?

A line segment

B line

C angle

D ray

GO ON

46. Emily has a sticker that looks like a quadrilateral that has 2 pairs of parallel sides and 4 equal sides. Which figure could be the shape of Emily's sticker?

A 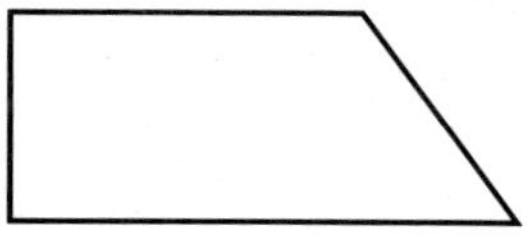

B 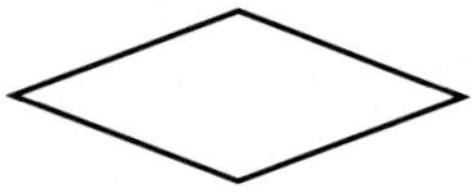

C 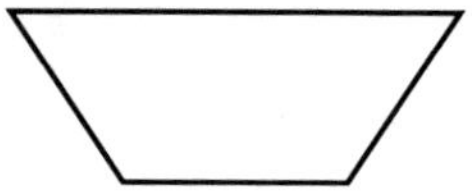

D 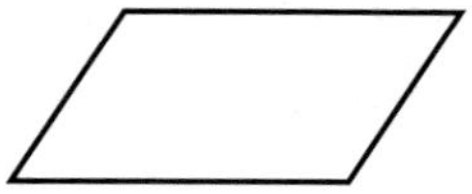

47. A sign is in the shape of an acute triangle. Which of the following could be the shape of the sign?

A 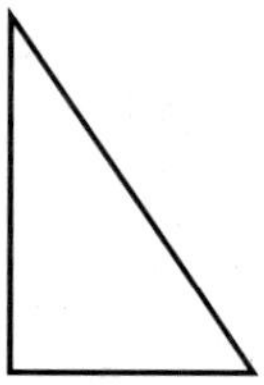

B 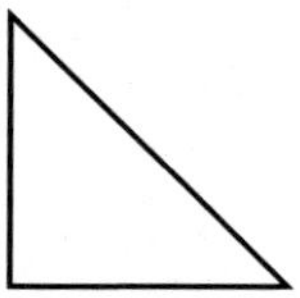

C 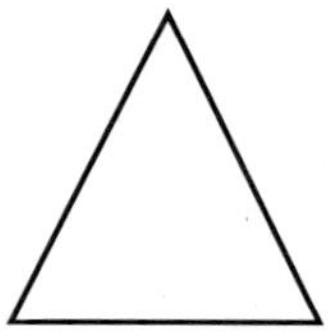

D 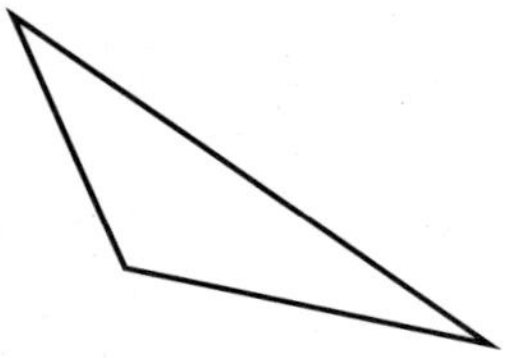

48. Jing read $\frac{1}{2}$ of his book on Saturday and $\frac{2}{3}$ of his book on Sunday. Which number is a common denominator for $\frac{1}{2}$ and $\frac{2}{3}$?

A 1

B 4

C 6

D 10

49. Jared fills an aquarium $\frac{3}{5}$ full of water. Which fraction is equivalent to $\frac{3}{5}$?

A $\frac{20}{38}$

B $\frac{8}{12}$

C $\frac{9}{15}$

D $\frac{11}{19}$

50. Nori bought $\frac{2}{3}$ pound of chicken salad and $\frac{3}{4}$ pound of tuna salad for a picnic. Which statement correctly compares the fractions?

A $\frac{2}{3} > \frac{3}{4}$

B $\frac{3}{4} > \frac{2}{3}$

C $\frac{2}{3} = \frac{3}{4}$

D $\frac{3}{4} < \frac{2}{3}$

GO ON

Name ____

51. Jeremy is finding the product of 29 and 42. Jeremy's answer is incorrect. What did Jeremy do wrong? What is the correct product?

$$\begin{array}{r} 29 \\ \times \quad 42 \\ \hline 580 \\ +\ 1160 \\ \hline 1740 \end{array}$$

Answer ____

____

____

52. Cassandra began her math homework at 5:45 P.M. She stopped at 6:30 P.M. How many degrees did the minute hand move while Cassandra was doing homework? Explain how you found your answer.

Answer ____

____

____

____

GO ON

53. Erin and two of her friends have 4 quarters, 3 dimes, and 4 nickels to spend. If Erin and her friends share the money equally, how much will each person get?

Show your work.

Answer _____

54. Steven works in a toy store that sells bags of blocks. He puts 12 blocks in each bag, and $\frac{9}{12}$ of the blocks are red.

PART A

If Steven makes 5 bags of blocks, how many red blocks does he need? Explain your answer.

Answer ____________________

____

____

PART B

Yesterday Steven used 63 red blocks to fill bags. How many blocks that are **not** red did he use to fill the bags? Explain your reasoning.

Answer

____

____

____

____

STOP

Name ______________________________

Choose the correct answer.

1. Juan plans to use a strategy to find 12×380. Which expression shows a strategy he could use?

   A $12 \times 0 \times 380$

   B $4 \times 4 \times 380$

   C $3 \times 4 \times 380$

   D $3 \times 4 \times 38$

2. Natalie manages a concert hall. She rented 312 chairs each week for the first 4 weeks in March. She also rented 267 chairs each week for the first 2 weeks of April. The rental company forgot to send 41 chairs. How many chairs did Natalie rent those 6 weeks?

   A 538

   B 1,692

   C 1,741

   D 1,823

3. A factory can make 3,848 pencils in one hour. Which is the **best** estimate of how many pencils can be made in 4 hours?

   A 160,000 pencils

   B 16,000 pencils

   C 12,000 pencils

   D 1,600 markers

4. Multiply 8×42. Which of the following statements is **true**?

   A The product is 324.

   B A reasonable estimate of the product is 320.

   C Using partial products, the products are 160 and 32.

   D Using regrouping, 16 ones are regrouped as 6 tens and 1 one.

5. Camden rides his bicycle $\frac{6}{10}$ mile to Dayton's house. Which fraction in hundredths is equal to $\frac{6}{10}$?

   A $\frac{6}{100}$

   B $\frac{60}{100}$

   C $\frac{600}{1,000}$

   D $\frac{600}{100}$

GO ON

Name ______________________________

6. Tony rode his bicycle $3\frac{7}{10}$ miles to school. What is this distance written as a decimal?

A 0.037 mile

B 0.37 mile

C 3.7 miles

D 37 miles

7. Craig hiked for $\frac{7}{10}$ mile and stopped to take pictures. Then he hiked for another $\frac{25}{100}$ mile. How far did he hike in all?

A $\frac{32}{100}$ mile

B $\frac{70}{100}$ mile

C $\frac{85}{100}$ mile

D $\frac{95}{100}$ mile

8. What is the measure of the unknown angle in the figure?

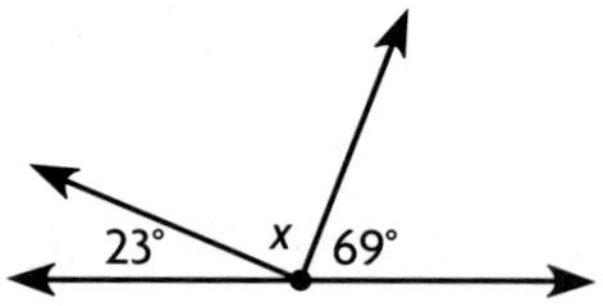

A 180°

B 92°

C 88°

D 44°

9. Caroline drew the angle below.

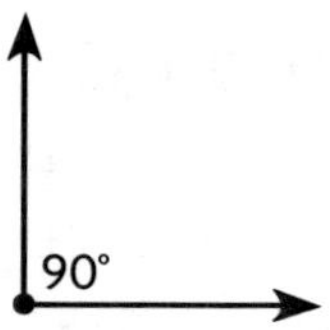

What name should Caroline give her angle?

A obtuse angle

B acute angle

C right angle

D straight angle

10. Eric put two angles together to form a straight angle. One angle measures 115°. What is the measure of the other angle?

A 65°

B 75°

C 85°

D 95°

GO ON

11. Which sum could represent the angle measures that make up a triangle?

A $170° + 120° + 70°$

B $150° + 40° + 10°$

C $110° + 50° + 20°$

D $40° + 40° + 10°$

12. Irene bought $\frac{9}{16}$ pound of wheat flour and $\frac{4}{16}$ pound of rye flour to use in a bread recipe. How much flour did Irene buy in all?

A $\frac{15}{16}$ pound

B $\frac{13}{16}$ pound

C $\frac{1}{2}$ pound

D $\frac{13}{32}$ pound

13. Which of the following shows the Commutative Property?

A $\frac{2}{7} + \left(\frac{5}{7} + \frac{3}{7}\right) = \left(\frac{2}{7} + \frac{5}{7}\right) + \frac{3}{7}$

B $\left(\frac{3}{5} + 1\frac{4}{5}\right) + 5\frac{2}{5} = \left(\frac{3}{5} + 1\frac{4}{5} + 5\frac{2}{5}\right)$

C $3\frac{1}{8} + \left(5\frac{1}{4} + 1\frac{7}{8}\right) = 3\frac{1}{8} + \left(1\frac{7}{8} + 5\frac{1}{4}\right)$

D $\left(\frac{1}{10} + \frac{3}{10}\right) + 6\frac{7}{10} = \frac{1}{10} + \left(\frac{3}{10} + 6\frac{7}{10}\right)$

14. One of the hiking trails at a state park is $\frac{14}{3}$ miles long. Which mixed number shows the length of the hiking trail?

A $4\frac{2}{3}$ miles

B $4\frac{1}{3}$ miles

C $3\frac{2}{3}$ miles

D $3\frac{1}{3}$ miles

15. Mark had $6\frac{3}{5}$ bottles of water for his track meet. When he finished, he had $3\frac{1}{5}$ bottles of water left. How many bottles of water did Mark use?

A $2\frac{4}{5}$

B $3\frac{2}{5}$

C 6

D $6\frac{3}{5}$

GO ON

16. Anna has 32 red beads, 16 blue beads, and 8 green beads. She wants to put an equal number of each kind of bead on necklaces she is making. How many of each kind of bead can Anna put on each necklace?

A 8

B 2, 4 or 8

C 2 or 4

D 1, 2, 4, or 8

17. Paula and Karen are playing a game. Paula counts by 4s. Karen counts by 5s. They try to pace the counting so they will say the first common number together. What is the first number they both say together?

A 20

B 15

C 12

D 5

18. Jeff's teacher writes a list of numbers on the board. She asks Jeff to circle the prime number. Which number should Jeff circle?

A 6

B 10

C 13

D 15

19. Ming writes a number pattern on a slip of paper and hands it to his friend Jack.

24, 21, 23, 20, 22, 19, 21, 18

Jack writes the next number in the pattern and hands the paper back to Ming. What number should Jack write?

A 19

B 20

C 21

D 22

20. Dawn's family is taking a 3-day vacation to visit her cousins. How many hours will they be away?

A 24 hours

B 36 hours

C 48 hours

D 72 hours

GO ON

21. The table shows a pattern for two units of customary capacity.

________	________
1	4
2	8
3	12
4	16

Which are the **best** labels for each column?

A Gallons, Cups

B Quarts, Cups

C Pints, Cups

D Cups, Fluid Ounces

22. Carlos and his family left for the amusement park at 8:35 A.M. The trip took 1 hour 55 minutes. What time did they arrive?

A 9.35 A.M.

B 10:15 A.M.

C 10:30 A.M.

D 10:45 A.M.

23. Sandy cut three pieces of yarn to use for her art project. One piece was 1 foot 8 inches long, one was 10 inches long, and one was 2 feet 6 inches long. How much yarn did Sandy use?

A 3 feet 12 inches

B 4 feet 10 inches

C 5 feet

D 5 feet 6 inches

24. A picture called a mosaic was made from 172,435 small clay tiles. What is the value of the digit 2 in 172,435?

A 200

B 2,000

C 20,000

D 200,000

25. Maya used number tiles to make the number 428,745. Then she changed two digits to make the number 427,845. Which statement about these numbers is correct?

A $428{,}745 < 427{,}845$

B $427{,}845 = 428{,}745$

C $427{,}845 > 428{,}745$

D $427{,}845 < 428{,}745$

GO ON

Name ______________________________

26. An amusement park had 56,437 visitors the first year and 48,319 visitors the second year it was open. What was the total number of visitors for both years?

A 114,756 visitors

B 104,756 visitors

C 104,746 visitors

D 94,746 visitors

27. A total of 937,428 visitors went to a theme park during June and July. If 431,529 visitors went to the theme park in June, how many visitors went to the theme park in July?

A 505,899

B 505,988

C 603,241

D 774,952

28. Roberta used 110 centimeters of ribbon to make a border around a rectangular card. The length of the card is 40 centimeters. How many centimeters is the width of the card?

A 30

B 25

C 15

D 10

29. Which of the following could be the dimensions of a rectangle with a perimeter of 70 inches?

A length: 15 inches; width: 15 inches

B length: 20 inches; width: 15 inches

C length: 30 inches; width: 10 inches

D length: 35 inches; width: 5 inches

30. Patrick drew this plan for a new walkway through his backyard.

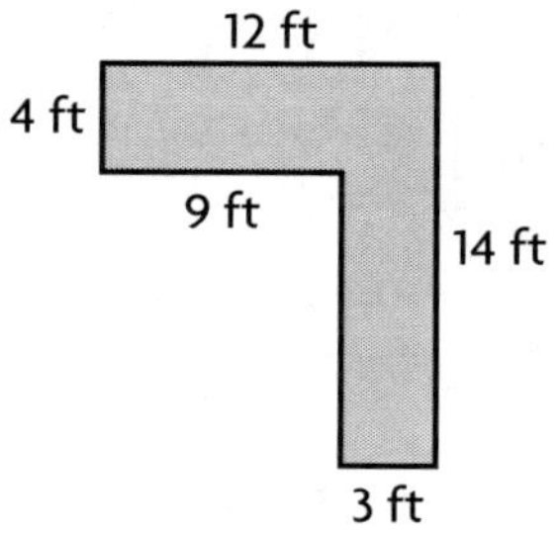

How many square feet of bricks will Patrick need to cover the walkway?

A 168 square feet

B 90 square feet

C 78 square feet

D 52 square feet

GO ON

31. Philip is making a poster that is 36 by 24 inches. He cuts a 5 x 12 rectangle in the poster. How much of the poster remains uncut?

A 140 square inches

B 704 square inches

C 804 square inches

D 864 square inches

32. Which shows the **best** estimate to use to find 43×78?

A $40 \times 70 = 2{,}800$

B $40 \times 80 = 3{,}200$

C $50 \times 70 = 3{,}500$

D $50 \times 80 = 4{,}000$

33. Chen can jump rope 60 times a minute. At that rate, how many jumps can he make in 9 minutes?

A 620

B 540

C 520

D 500

34. Marjorie's customers bought 94 bouquets at her flower shop for $14 each. What is the total amount customers paid for the bouquets?

A $1,216

B $1,306

C $1,316

D $1,416

35. Lonnie works weekends at his uncle's apple orchid. He has 47 baskets of apples to pack. Each basket holds 35 apples. How many apples in all will Lonnie pack?

A 1,745

B 1,715

C 1,645

D 1,445

GO ON

36. Matt is making a picture frame from a piece of wood trim that is $\frac{27}{8}$ feet long. How can Matt rename the fraction as a mixed number?

A $3\frac{3}{8}$

B $2\frac{3}{8}$

C $2\frac{1}{4}$

D $1\frac{3}{8}$

37. Suki named a fraction that was **not** a multiple of $\frac{3}{4}$. Which fraction could she have named?

A $\frac{6}{4}$

B $\frac{9}{4}$

C $\frac{10}{4}$

D $\frac{12}{4}$

38. Larry rides his bike $\frac{5}{6}$ mile 4 times a week. How far does Larry ride his bike each week?

A $3\frac{1}{3}$ miles

B $3\frac{2}{3}$ miles

C 4 miles

D 20 miles

39. Maria used $4\frac{1}{6}$ gallons of paint on her living room walls. She used 3 times as much paint for her kitchen and dining room walls. How many gallons of paint did Maria use for the kitchen and dining room walls?

A $12\frac{3}{6}$

B 11

C $9\frac{2}{6}$

D 7

40. Rachel and her three sisters divided 3,084 stickers equally. About how many stickers did each girl receive?

A 500

B 800

C 1,000

D 2,000

GO ON

41. The art teacher needs 70 markers for her classes. The markers come in packages of 15. How many packages of markers will the art teacher need to buy?

A 5

B 4

C 3

D 2

42. A movie theater sold 2,604 tickets in 6 days. They sold the same number of tickets each day. How many tickets did the theater sell each day?

A 404

B 434

C 443

D 534

43. A pencil company packs pencils in boxes of 8. How many boxes can they pack with 32,000 pencils?

A 40,000

B 4,000

C 400

D 40

44. Brad drew the figure below.

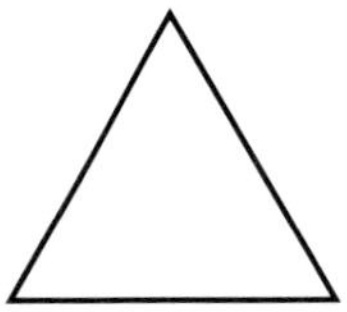

How many lines of symmetry does the figure have?

A 4

B 3

C 2

D 1

45. Connie drew the figure below as an example for her classmate.

Which of the following terms **best** describes the figure Connie drew?

A line segment

B line

C angle

D ray

GO ON

46. Kelly has a sticker that looks like a quadrilateral that has 2 pairs of parallel sides, 2 pairs of equal sides, and 4 right angles. Which figure could be the shape of Kelly's sticker?

A 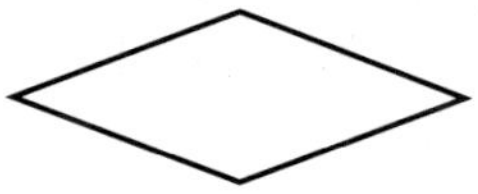

B 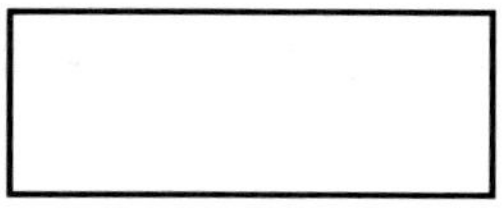

C 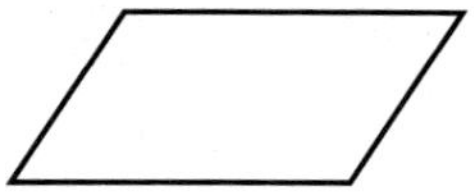

D 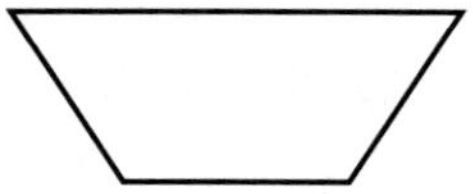

47. A flag is in the shape of a right triangle. Which of the following could be the shape of the flag?

A 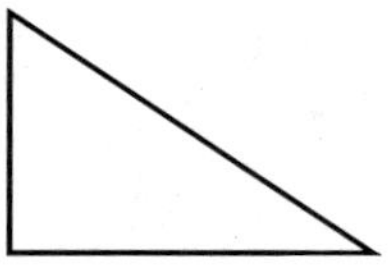

B 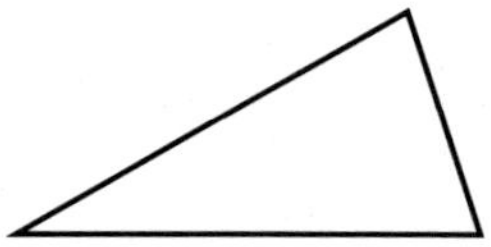

C 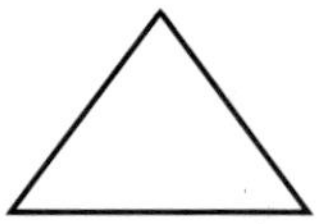

D 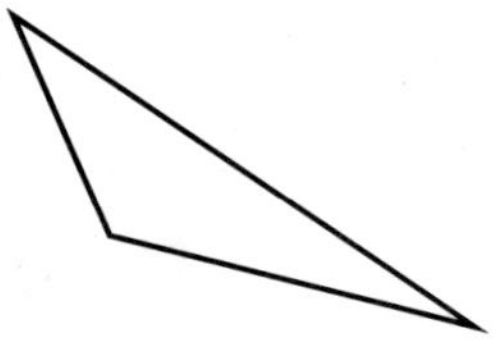

48. Andy walked $\frac{3}{4}$ of a mile to the post office and another $\frac{1}{2}$ mile to the supermarket. Which number is a common denominator for $\frac{3}{4}$ and $\frac{1}{2}$?

A 10

B 9

C 6

D 4

49. Todd fills an aquarium $\frac{7}{9}$ full of water. Which fraction is equivalent to $\frac{7}{9}$?

A $\frac{26}{55}$

B $\frac{8}{15}$

C $\frac{14}{18}$

D $\frac{13}{10}$

50. Anita mixes $\frac{3}{5}$ pound of peanuts with $\frac{3}{8}$ pound of raisins to make a snack. Which statement correctly compares the fractions?

A $\frac{3}{8} = \frac{3}{5}$

B $\frac{3}{8} > \frac{3}{5}$

C $\frac{3}{5} > \frac{3}{8}$

D $\frac{3}{5} < \frac{3}{8}$

GO ON

Name ___________________________________

51. Christian is finding the product of 32 and 43. Christian's answer is incorrect. What did Christian do wrong? What is the correct product?

$$\begin{array}{r} 32 \\ \times \quad 43 \\ \hline 960 \\ +\ 1280 \\ \hline 2240 \end{array}$$

Answer ___________________________________

____

____

52. Alicia began her math homework at 5:45 P.M. She stopped at 6:15 P.M. How many degrees did the minute hand move while Alicia was doing homework? Explain how you found your answer.

Answer ___________________________________

____

____

____

GO ON

53. Jessica and two of her friends have 5 quarters, 6 dimes, and 5 nickels to spend. If Jessica and her friends share the money equally, how much will each person get?

Show your work.

Answer ______

54. Michael works in a toy store that sells bags of blocks. He puts 10 blocks in each bag, and $\frac{6}{10}$ of the blocks are blue.

PART A

If Michael makes 5 bags of blocks, how many blue blocks does he need? Explain your answer.

Answer ______________________

____

____

PART B

Yesterday Michael used 48 blue blocks to fill bags. How many blocks that are **not** blue did he use to fill the bags? Explain your reasoning.

Answer ______________________

____

____

____

STOP

Name ______________________________

Choose the correct answer.

1. Members of a stamp-collecting club have 213,094 stamps altogether. What is 213,094 written in word form?

A two hundred thirteen, ninety-four

B two hundred thirteen thousand, ninety-four

C two hundred thirteen thousand, nine hundred four

D two hundred thirteen thousand, four

2. The surface area of Lake Superior is 31,700 square miles. The surface area of Lake Michigan is 22,278 square miles. What is the total surface area of both lakes?

A 9,422 square miles

B 22,595 square miles

C 53,278 square miles

D 53,978 square miles

3. The population of Miguel's hometown is 23,718. What is 23,718 rounded to the nearest ten thousand?

A 20,000

B 23,700

C 24,000

D 30,000

4. Darla copies her uncle's address and phone number into her contact list. His area code is 775. His ZIP code is 89507. Which statement about the value of the 5 in 77<u>5</u> and 89,<u>5</u>07 is true?

A It is the same in both numbers.

B It is 10 times as great in the ZIP code than it is in the area code.

C It is 100 times as great in the ZIP code than it is in the area code.

D It is 10 times as great in the area code than it is in the ZIP code.

GO ON

5. A theme park had 674,989 visitors in June and 812,383 visitors in July. In August, the park had **more** visitors than in June, but **fewer** visitors than in July. Which of the following could be the number of visitors in August?

A 544,989

B 646,844

C 765,124

D 820,486

6. The number of inner tubes rented at the river this year **increased by** 1,009 over last year. The number of inner tubes rented last year was 4,286. How many inner tubes were rented this year?

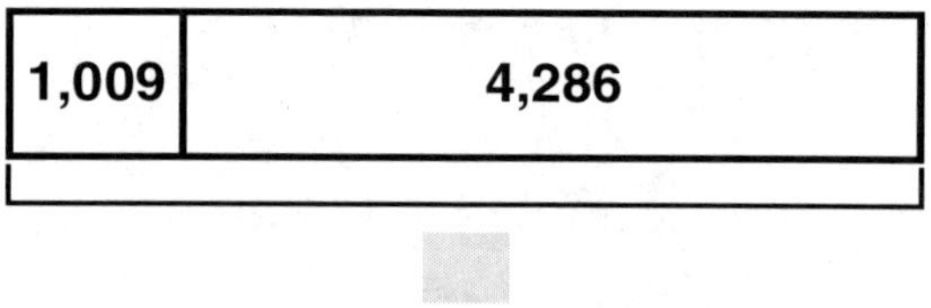

A 3,277

B 4,395

C 5,285

D 5,295

7. Arizona has a land area of 113,998 square miles. Wyoming has a land area of 97,818 square miles. How much **greater** is the area, in square miles, of Arizona than the area of Wyoming?

A 16,180

B 26,180

C 106,180

D 211,816

8. What is another way to show 106,423?

A 100,000 + 60,000 + 400 + 20 + 3

B one hundred six thousand, four hundred three

C one hundred sixty thousand, four hundred twenty

D 1 hundred thousand + 6 thousands + 4 hundreds + 2 tens + 3 ones

GO ON

9. The total season attendance for a professional football team's home games, rounded to the nearest ten thousand, was 710,000. Which number could be the exact attendance?

A 700,987

B 701,752

C 706,797

D 715,006

10. A car wash cleaned 97,612 cars in 2010 and 121,048 cars in 2011. What is the total number of cars washed in 2010 and 2011?

A 109,716

B 109,760

C 118,650

D 218,660

11. The attendance at a rock concert was 79,408 people. What is the value of the digit 4 in 79,408?

A 40

B 400

C 4,000

D 40,000

12. A total of 543,718 visitors went to a theme park during August and September. If 321,654 visitors went to the theme park in August, how many visitors went to the theme park in September?

A 211,074

B 222,064

C 222,164

D 865,372

GO ON

Name ________________________________

13. A factory produces between 320,000 and 340,000 clay pots each day.

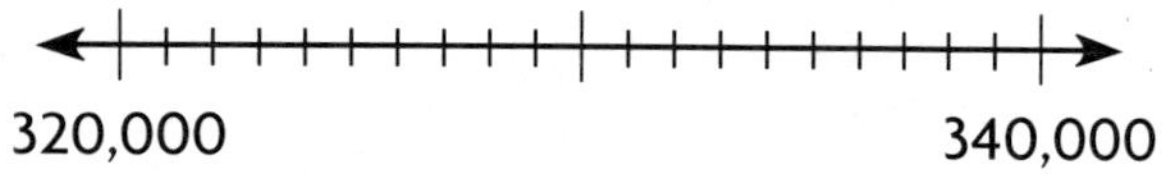

Which statement is **true**?

A 320,000 > 329,000

B 330,000 < 320,000

C 329,000 > 320,000

D 340,000 < 329,000

14. Mr. Rey and Ms. Klein both took long car trips. Mr. Rey drove 2,178 miles. Ms. Klein drove 1,830 miles. How much farther did Mr. Rey drive on his trip?

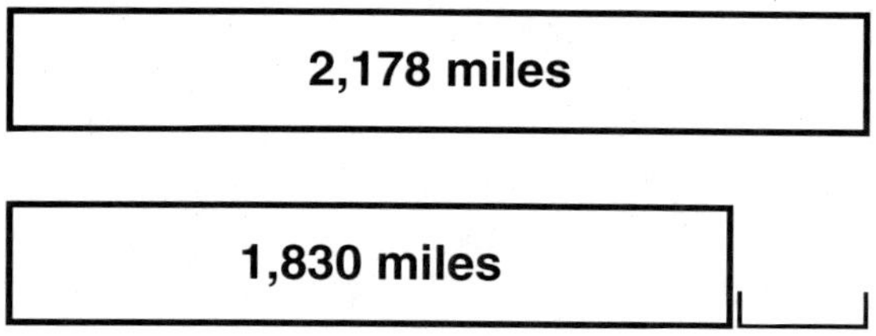

A 348 miles

B 748 miles

C 1,348 miles

D 4,008 miles

15. The tollbooth records show that 105,076 cars passed through the toll plaza on Saturday. What is the expanded form of 105,076?

A 10,000 + 5,000 + 70 + 6

B 100,000 + 5,000 + 60 + 7

C 100,000 + 50,000 + 7 + 6

D 100,000 + 5,000 + 70 + 6

16. Michigan State and Wayne State are two large colleges in Michigan. Michigan State has 45,166 students. Wayne State has 32,160 students. How many **more** students go to Michigan State?

A 3,006

B 13,000

C 13,006

D 13,326

GO ON

17. Last week, about 456,900 viewers watched a television show on the Egyptian pyramids. What is the **greatest** whole number that rounds to 456,900?

A 456,850

B 456,949

C 460,000

D 466,000

18. Brenda used number tiles to make the number 735,512. Frank used number tiles to make the number 734,512. Which statement about these numbers is correct?

A 735,512 > 734,512

B 735,512 < 734,512

C 735,512 = 734,512

D 734,512 > 735,512

19. A science museum has collected a total of 8,536 plant fossils. They have also collected 3,855 animal fossils. Use the bar model to find the total number of fossils the museum has.

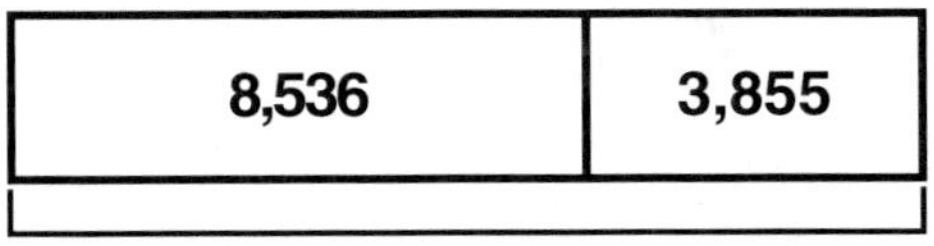

A 12,481

B 12,391

C 11,381

D 4,681

20. Last season, 57,690 fans went to football games at Oneida High School. This season 54,083 fans went to the games. What is the total number of fans who went to Oneida High School football games during both seasons?

A 3,607

B 110,673

C 111,773

D 112,673

GO ON

21. Which number will make the comparison **true**?

807,058 > ______

A 800,758

B 807,085

C 870,058

D 870,508

22. Francisco is placing an order for bookplates so he can label the library books. There are 47,482 books that need labels. What is 47,482 rounded to the nearest ten thousand?

A 40,000

B 47,000

C 48,000

D 50,000

23. Carson made a four-digit number with a 4 in the thousands place, a 4 in the ones places, a 5 in the tens place, and a 6 in the hundreds place. What was the number?

A 4,456

B 4,546

C 4,645

D 4,654

24. A desktop computer that Ryan likes costs $1,275. A laptop model of the same computer costs $1,648. How much **more** does the laptop cost?

A $473

B $433

C $373

D $333

25. The table shows the number of votes for each of three candidates during an election.

Election Results

Candidate	Number of Votes
Clark	1,721
Perez	11,721
Jones	11,127

What list shows these numbers in order from **least** to **greatest?**

A 11,721; 11,127; 1,721

B 1,721; 11,127; 11,721

C 1,721; 11,721; 11,127

D 11,127; 1,721; 11,721

GO ON

Name ______________________________

26. An ice-skating competition lasted three days. Day one had an attendance of 16,390 people. Day two had an attendance of 16,550 people. Day three had an attendance of 16,237 people. Use pictures, words, or numbers to put the days in order from least attendance to greatest attendance. Which day had the least attendance?

Show your work.

Answer ______________________________

27. Tanya, Will, and Juan are playing a game online. Juan scores 101,473 points. Tanya scores 9,879 **fewer** points than Juan, and Will scores 9,853 **more** points than Tanya. What is Will's score?

Show your work.

Answer ______ points

28. The table shows recent population data from Fresno, California.

Population of Fresno, CA			
Age in years	**Population**	**Age in years**	**Population**
Under 5	43,911	20 to 34	119,388
5 to 9	40,087	35 to 49	89,416
10 to 14	39,634	50 to 64	72,261
15 to 19	43,867	65 and over	46,101

How many children are under 10 years old?

Show your work.

Answer _____ children

GO ON

29. Leslie wrote the **greatest** number that can be made using each of these digits exactly once.

6	2	4	7	9	1

PART A

What was Leslie's number? How do you know this is the greatest possible number for these digits?

Answer ______________________________

PART B

What is the **least** number that can be made using each digit exactly once? Why is the value of the 4 greater than the value of the 6?

Answer ______________________________

STOP

Name ______________________________

Choose the correct answer.

1. An art store has 5 boxes of brushes. Each box contains 298 brushes. Which expression shows a strategy for finding the product of 5×298?

A $5 \times (300 + 2)$

B $5 \times (300 - 2)$

C $5 \times (300 \times 3)$

D $5 \times (200 - 98)$

2. Which equation is **true**?

A $4 \times 938 = 3{,}652$

B $6 \times 723 = 4{,}228$

C $7 \times 3{,}249 = 22{,}743$

D $9 \times 2{,}640 = 23{,}769$

3. Mindy picked 4 times as many daisies as tulips for a flower bouquet. She picked a total of 20 flowers. How many **more** daisies than tulips did she pick?

A 4

B 5

C 12

D 16

4. Carrie manages a catering company. She rented 325 chairs each week for the first two weeks of May. Carrie rented 750 chairs each week for the first two weeks of April. The chair rental company forgot to send 23 chairs. How many chairs did Carrie receive in those 4 weeks?

A 972

B 1,038

C 1,964

D 2,127

5. Madeline has 32 shells. This is 4 times as many shells as Rob has. Madeline made a model to compare the numbers of shells they have.

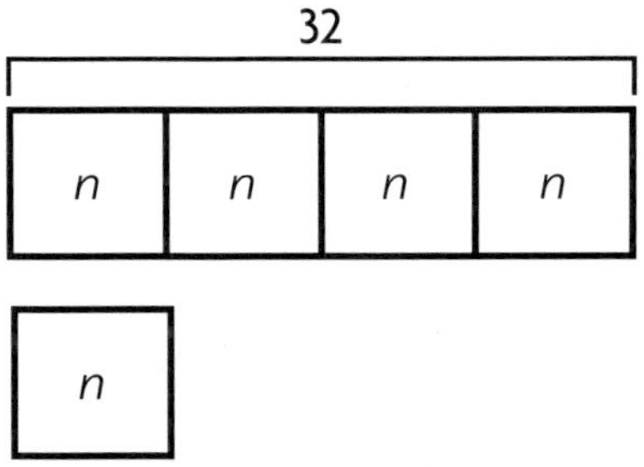

Which equation represents how to find the value of n?

A $32 = n + 4$

B $32 = 4 \times n$

C $32 + 4 = n$

D $32 \times 4 = n$

GO ON

6. Mr. Richards travels 163 miles each week for work. How far does he travel in 4 weeks for work?

A 442 miles

B 452 miles

C 642 miles

D 652 miles

7. Hideki is collecting pennies. Each month in May, June, and July, he put 200 pennies in a jug. He put 300 pennies in the jug in August and 300 in September. How many pennies did Hideki put in the jug between May and September?

A 600

B 1,200

C 6,000

D 12,000

8. Gerard has 128 songs stored on his portable music player. He wants to triple his music library. Gerard makes a model to help him find how many songs he will have in his music library.

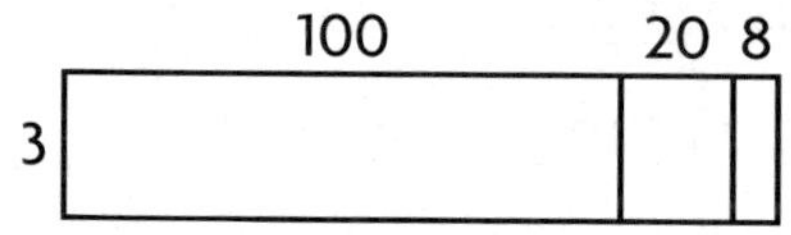

How many songs will Gerard have?

A 131

B 328

C 384

D 3,128

9. Dane has a stamp collection. In one book he has 6 pages with 15 stamps on each page. In another book he has 9 pages with 20 stamps on each page. He gives 25 stamps to a friend. Which of these equations can Dane use to find how many stamps he has left?

A $6 \times 15 \times 9 \times 20 - 25 = n$

B $6 \times 15 + 9 \times 20 - 25 = n$

C $6 + 15 \times 9 + 20 - 25 = n$

D $6 + 15 \times 9 \times 20 + 25 = n$

GO ON

Name ______________________________

10. Multiply 6 × 64. Which statement is true?

A The product is 384.

B A reasonable estimate of the product is 500.

C Using partial products, the products are 240 and 36.

D Using regrouping, 24 ones are regrouped as 4 tens and 2 ones.

11. A factory produces 2,354 hammers every hour. Which expression can be used to find how many hammers the factory produces in 3 hours?

A $(3 \times 2{,}000) + 354$

B $(3 \times 2{,}000) + (3 \times 300) + 54$

C $(3 \times 2{,}000) + (3 \times 300) + (3 \times 50) + (3 \times 4)$

D $(3 \times 2{,}000) + (300 + 50 + 4)$

12. It costs 8,355 points to build each school in the computer game *Town Planning*. How much does it cost to build 6 schools?

A 50,130 points

B 47,649 points

C 34,521 points

D 28,743 points

13. Beth travels 244 miles every week. She says she will travel 2,196 miles if she travels the same number of miles for the next 9 weeks.

Which statement **best** describes the reasonableness of Beth's answer?

A The answer is reasonable because it is close to the estimate of 9 × 2,000.

B The answer is reasonable because it is close to the estimate of 9 × 300.

C The answer is reasonable because it is close to the estimate of 3,000.

D The answer is reasonable because it is between the estimates of 1,800 and 2,700.

GO ON

14. Zeke made this model to find the product of a 3-digit number and a 1-digit number.

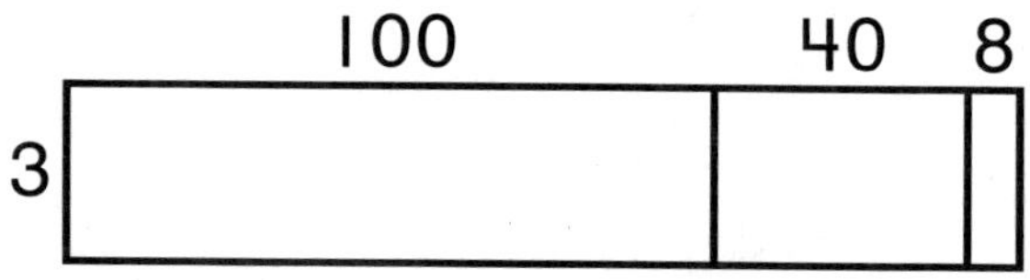

Which multiplication sentence represents Zeke's model?

A $3 \times 184 = 552$

B $3 \times 140 = 420$

C $3 \times 108 = 324$

D $3 \times 148 = 444$

15. Jerome has 5 albums with 18 baseball cards in each. His friend gives him 7 packages of baseball cards with 13 cards in each. If Jerome buys another 10 baseball cards, how many baseball cards will he have?

A 53

B 181

C 191

D 483

16. Brandon has 4,350 digital photos saved on his computer. Linda has 3 times as many photos saved on her computer as Brandon has. How many digital photos does Linda have saved on her computer?

A 12,050

B 12,250

C 12,950

D 13,050

17. Julia has 24 baseball cards in 6 packs. She writes that 24 is 4 times as many as 6. Which other comparison sentence can she write in her record book to show the comparison?

A 6 more than 4 is 24.

B 6 is 4 times as many as 24.

C 24 is 6 times as many as 4.

D 4 is 6 times as many as 24.

GO ON

Name ______________________________

18. A large truck that can carry up to 168 boxes in a single trip will make 6 trips in one day. Which expression shows how to multiply 6×168 by using place value and expanded form?

A $(6 \times 100) + (6 \times 60) + (6 \times 8)$

B $(6 \times 800) + (6 \times 60) + (6 \times 1)$

C $(6 \times 100) + (6 \times 60)$

D $(6 \times 168) + (6 \times 16) + (6 \times 1)$

19. A black bear has a mass of about 135 kilograms. Which is the **best** estimate of the mass of 3 black bears?

A less than 300 kilograms

B between 300 and 600 kilograms

C between 600 and 900 kilograms

D more than 900 kilograms

20. Carl plans to use a strategy to find 28×250. Which expression shows a strategy he could use?

A $5 \times 6 \times 250$

B $4 \times 7 \times 25$

C $7 \times 4 \times 250$

D $28 \times 0 \times 250$

21. Sara's mom bought tickets to the Philadelphia Zoo. She bought 6 tickets. Each ticket cost $18. What was the total cost of the tickets?

A $32

B $68

C $108

D $114

GO ON

22. Maria wrote this pattern in her math notebook.

$8 \times 5 = 40$
$8 \times 50 = 400$
$8 \times 500 = 4,000$
$8 \times \square = 40,000$

What is the unknown number in Maria's pattern?

A 50,000

B 5,000

C 500

D 5

23. A store has 2 times as many hooded sweatshirts as crewneck sweatshirts. The total number of sweatshirts is 36. How many hooded sweatshirts does the store have?

A 6

B 12

C 18

D 24

24. Lana bought party favors at the store for the school's 6th grade graduation party. Lana bought 7 bags of party hats with 12 hats in each bag. Lana also bought 4 bags of horns with 24 horns in each bag. How many **more** horns than party hats did Lana buy?

A 12

B 16

C 20

D 24

25. There is a plant sale at school. The price for each plant is $7. Which expression can be used to show how much money the school will make if it sells 325 plants?

A $(7 \times 30) + (7 \times 5) + (7 \times 2)$

B $(7 \times 50) + (7 \times 30) + (7 \times 7)$

C $(7 \times 300) + (7 \times 20) + (7 \times 5)$

D $(7 \times 300) + (7 \times 50) + (7 \times 2)$

GO ON

Name ______________________________

26. Use the Distributive Property to model the product 4×16 on the grid. What is the product?

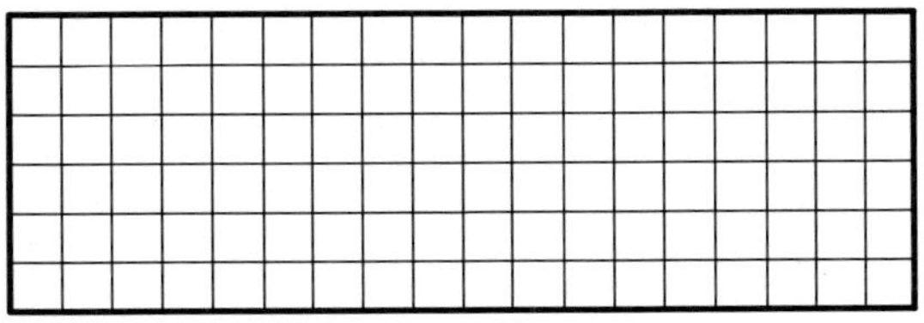

Answer __________

27. What is 9×503? Choose a strategy to find the answer and explain why it works best with the factors.

Answer ______________________________

____

____

28. Heidi's mom made flower arrangements for a party. She made 4 times as many rose arrangements as tulip arrangements. Heidi's mom made a total of 40 arrangements. How many flower arrangements of each type did Heidi's mom make? Complete the bar model.

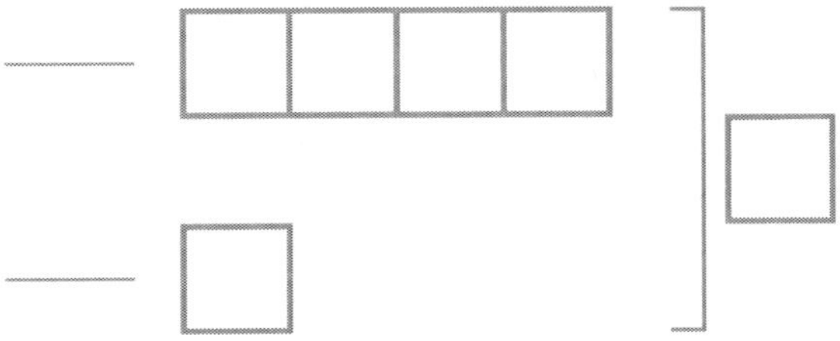

Answer ______________________________

GO ON

Name ______________________________

29. Kris and Julio played a card game. Together, they scored 36 points in one game. Kris scored 2 times as many points as Julio.

PART A

How many points did Kris and Julio each score? Write an equation and solve.

Show your work.

Answer Kris: ___ points, Julio: ___ points

PART B

Suppose Kris and Julio played the card game again. Together, they scored 40 points in one game. This time, Julio scored 3 times as many points as Kris. How many points did Kris and Julio each score in this game?

Show your work.

Answer Julio: ___ points, Kris: ___ points

STOP

Name ______________________________

Choose the correct answer.

1. Which shows the **best** estimate to use to find 52×67?

   A $50 \times 60 = 3{,}000$

   B $50 \times 70 = 3{,}500$

   C $55 \times 65 = 3{,}375$

   D $52 \times 100 = 5{,}200$

2. Mr. Thomas places orders for pencils with the school emblem. The order includes 15 boxes of pencils, and each box holds 25 pencils. How many pencils does Mr. Thomas order?

   A 40

   B 42

   C 225

   D 375

3. There are 28 boxes of pens in Mr. Gardner's supply cabinet. Each box contains 100 pens. How many pens are in the supply cabinet?

   A 28

   B 280

   C 2,800

   D 28,000

4. Doug rents a kayak for 12 days. The rental charge is \$18 per day. Which is the **best** estimate for the total cost of the kayak rental?

   A about \$400

   B about \$200

   C about \$160

   D about \$120

GO ON

5. In July, traffic officers wrote an average of 34 tickets each day. In August, they wrote an average of 47 tickets each day. How many more tickets did traffic officers write in August than in July? (Hint: July and August have 31 days each.)

A 403

B 1,045

C 1,457

D 2,511

6. Gabe runs on a treadmill for 45 minutes every morning. His body uses about 12 calories per minute to keep him moving. How many calories does Gabe use during his run?

A 135

B 440

C 540

D 850

7. Which equation is **not** correct?

A $60 \times 30 = 180$

B $75 \times 10 = 750$

C $14 \times 20 = 280$

D $50 \times 50 = 2{,}500$

8. Alex has 21 marbles. Zach has 19 times as many marbles as Alex. How many marbles does Zach have?

A 380

B 399

C 400

D 420

GO ON

Name ______________________________

9. Students arranged 13 chairs in each of 32 rows for the school play. What is the total number of chairs the students arranged?

A 300

B 320

C 384

D 416

10. A youth center sold raffle tickets to raise money for supplies. They sold 62 books of raffle tickets for $18 each. How much money did the youth center raise?

A $1,116

B $1,016

C $816

D $558

11. Grandma has 30 pages in her photo album. Each page has 2 rows with 5 pictures in each row. How many pictures are in Grandma's album?

A 10

B 60

C 150

D 300

12. Mr. Yu travels 46 miles for work every week. He worked 42 weeks last year. Which is the **best** estimate of the number of miles he traveled for work last year?

A about 1,000 miles

B about 2,000 miles

C about 8,000 miles

D about 10,000 miles

13. Ben swam laps in a pool nonstop for 11 minutes. There are 60 seconds in 1 minute. What is the total number of seconds Ben swam?

A 6,600 seconds

B 710 seconds

C 660 seconds

D 600 seconds

GO ON

14. Maria packed 24 bags of dog treats for the animal shelter. She put 16 dog treats in each bag. What is the total number of dog treats Maria packed?

A 168

B 240

C 384

D 624

15. Customers bought 52 shirts for $28 each. What is the total amount they paid for the shirts?

A $1,040

B $1,046

C $1,440

D $1,456

16. Rosa's vegetable garden has 15 rows of 32 corn plants each.

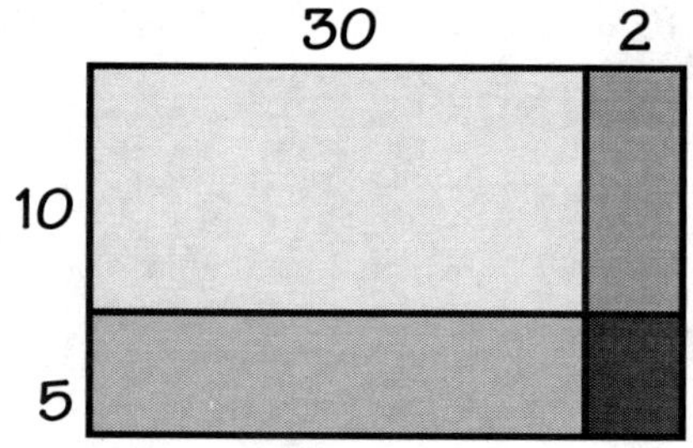

How many corn plants are in Rosa's vegetable garden?

A 480

B 465

C 450

D 300

17. Cat cages cost $27 each. A cat hospital bought 12 new cages. Which is the **best** estimate of the total cost of the new cages?

A $600

B $300

C $270

D $200

GO ON

18. Bill and Alyssa helped pack books to donate to a charity. Bill packed 28 boxes with 30 books in each box. Alyssa packed 31 boxes with 25 books in each box. How many **more** books did Bill pack?

A 3

B 65

C 118

D 230

19. What is 51×13?

A 650

B 663

C 750

D 765

20. People can join a skating club by paying $40 a year. The club had 67 members this year. How much money in all did the skating club collect from members this year?

A $268

B $2,680

C $3,220

D $26,800

21. There are 68 students in the book club. Each student reads 14 books during summer vacation. How many books do the students read in all during summer vacation?

A 340

B 922

C 952

D 1,020

GO ON

22. Some students are reorganizing supplies in the art room. They put 25 crayons in each of 24 boxes. What is the total number of crayons the students put into boxes?

A 760

B 600

C 582

D 200

23. On Friday, 17 buses left the bus station. Each bus carried a full load of 53 passengers. Which is the **best** way to estimate the total number of passengers who left the bus station that day?

A $10 \times 50 = 500$

B $10 \times 60 = 600$

C $20 \times 50 = 1{,}000$

D $20 \times 60 = 1{,}200$

24. Jevonne lives in a large apartment building. It has 17 floors. Each floor has 8 apartments. Each apartment has 6 rooms. What is the total number of rooms in the apartment building?

A 996

B 816

C 238

D 150

25. There are 96 word search puzzles in a puzzle book. Each puzzle has 22 words. How many words in all does the puzzle book have?

A 384

B 2,002

C 2,012

D 2,112

GO ON

Name ______________________________

26. Steve and Bradley are finding the product of 25 and 21. Both of their answers are incorrect. What did they do wrong, and what is the correct product?

Steve	Bradley
25	25
× 21	× 21
250	400
+ 500	10
750	20
	+ 5
	435

Answer ______________________________

____

27. The school principal orders 6 new chalkboards for each grade. There are 3 grades in the school. Each new chalkboard costs $98. What is the total cost for the new chalkboards?

Show your work.

Answer ________

28. Albert made this model to find the product of 43 × 28. His model is incorrect. What did Albert do wrong?

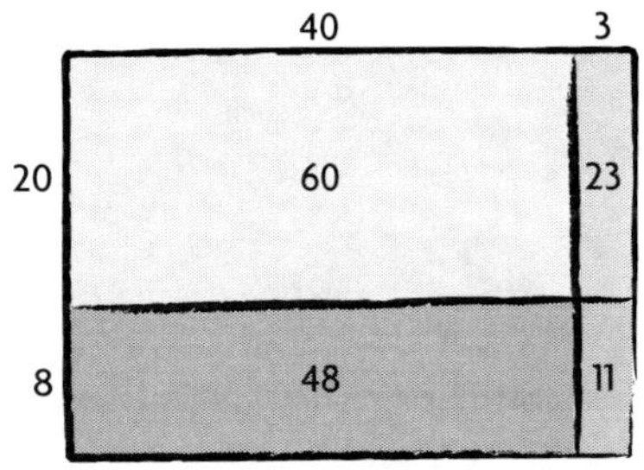

$43 \times 28 = 142$

Answer ______________________________

____

____

GO ON

Name ______________________________

29. Mr. Burns's class is taking a field trip to the planetarium. The trip will cost $27 for each student. There are 18 students in his class.

PART A

What is the estimated total cost of the field trip by rounding each factor and by using compatible numbers?

Show your work.

Answer _____ by rounding each factor and _____ by using compatible numbers

PART B

What do you think is the better estimate?

Show your work.

Answer ______________________________
____

STOP

Name ______________________________

Choose the correct answer.

1. There are 9 showings of a film about endangered species at the science museum. A total of 458 people saw the film. About how many people were at each showing?

   A about 40

   B about 50

   C about 60

   D about 90

2. On Friday, 278 fourth graders went on a field trip to the Arizona State Museum. The staff divided them into 7 tour groups. Which is the **best** estimate of the number of students in each tour group?

   A 50

   B 40

   C 20

   D 7

3. Zack needs to divide these base-ten blocks into 3 equal groups.

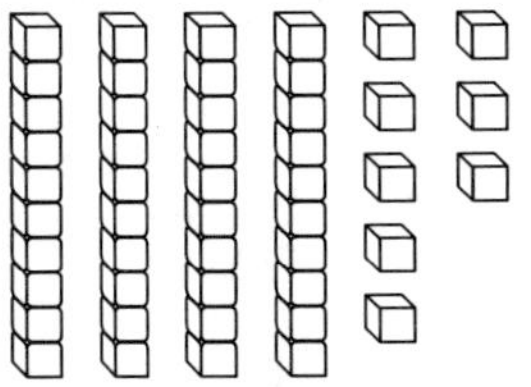

   Which model shows how many are in each equal group?

   A

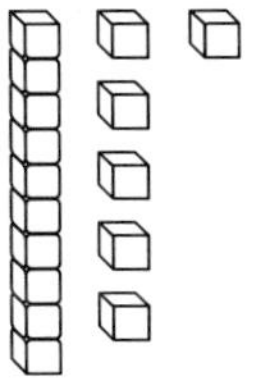

   B

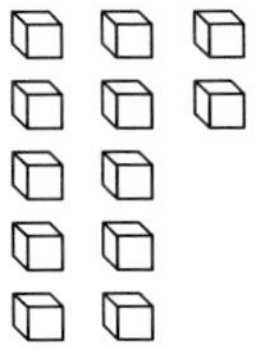

   C

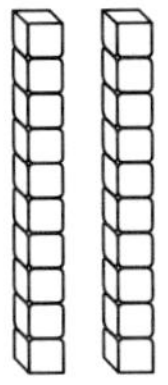

   D

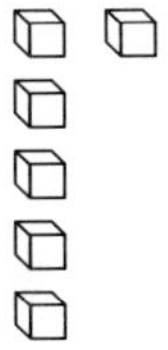

4. A park guide plans the swan boat rides for 40 people. Each boat can carry 6 people at a time. What is the **best** way to interpret the remainder of $40 \div 6$ in this situation so that everyone gets a ride?

   A Write the remainder as a fraction.

   B Use the remainder as the answer.

   C Use only the quotient.

   D Add 1 to the quotient.

GO ON

5. There are 48 people waiting for a fishing tour. Each tour boat can hold 12 passengers. Which number sentence can be used to find how many boats will be needed?

A $48 - 12 - 12 - 12 - 12 = 0$

B $12 + 48 = 60$

C $48 - 12 = 36$

D $48 - 24 = 24$

6. Which division sentence has a remainder?

A $32 \div 4$

B $41 \div 3$

C $48 \div 8$

D $63 \div 9$

7. Keith wants to fill 9 pages of his photo album with the same number of photographs on each page. If he has 117 photographs, how many photographs will he put on each page?

A 8

B 13

C 17

D 23

8. Which is a way to use the Distributive Property to break apart the dividend to find the quotient $128 \div 4$?

A $(104 \div 2) + (24 \div 2)$

B $(101 \div 1) + (27 \div 3)$

C $(64 \div 4) + (64 \div 4)$

D $(12 \div 4) + (28 \div 4)$

GO ON

Name ____________________

9. Which quotient is equal to 600?

A $6{,}000 \div 3$

B $1{,}200 \div 2$

C $420 \div 7$

D $180 \div 3$

10. Colin wants to distribute 186 of his baseball trading cards equally among 9 of his friends. In which place is the first digit of the quotient?

A ones

B tens

C hundreds

D thousands

11. Which number sentence is **not** true?

A $200 \div 5 = 50$

B $400 \div 8 = 50$

C $2{,}000 \div 4 = 500$

D $4{,}000 \div 8 = 500$

12. Between which two numbers would you find the quotient of $87 \div 5$?

A between 5 and 10

B between 10 and 15

C between 15 and 20

D between 20 and 25

13. Jessie has 160 rubber bracelets. She arranges the bracelets in piles of 40. Which model shows $160 \div 40$?

A

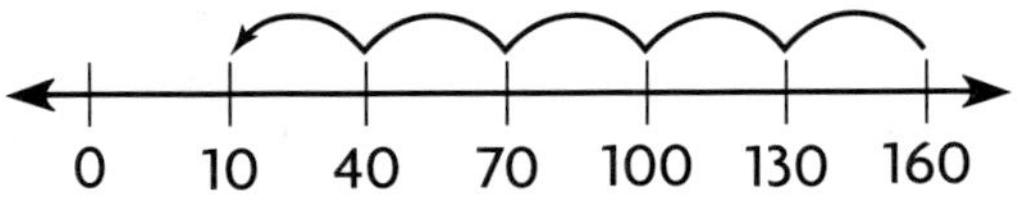

B

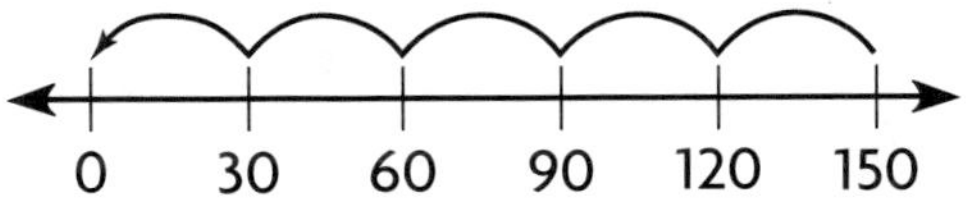

C

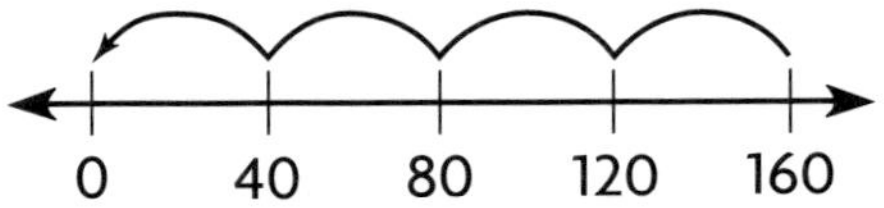

D

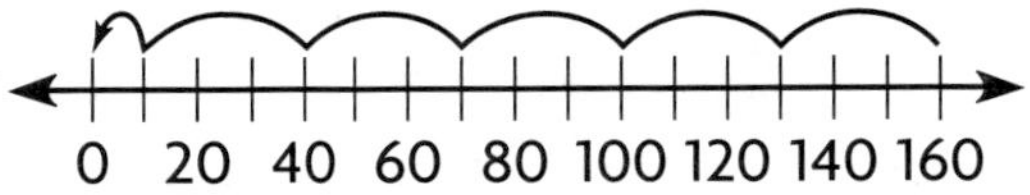

GO ON

14. Ursula bought 9 dozen gauze pads for the health office. The gauze pads were divided equally into 4 boxes. How many gauze pads are in each box?

A 108

B 36

C 27

D 24

15. A toy manufacturer has 627 yo-yos to divide equally among 3 stores. How many yo-yos will each store receive?

A 29

B 209

C 219

D 309

16. There are 112 seats in the school auditorium. There are 7 seats in each row. There are 70 people seated, filling up full rows of seats. How many rows are empty?

A 6

B 10

C 16

D 28

17. Nolan divides his 88 toy cars into boxes. Each box holds 9 cars. How many boxes does Nolan need to store all of his cars?

A 7

B 9

C 10

D 12

GO ON

Name ______________________________

18. Popcorn was donated for the school fair by 3 different popcorn vendors. They donated a total of 636 bags of popcorn. If each vendor donated the same number of bags, how many bags of popcorn did each vendor donate?

A 112

B 202

C 210

D 212

19. Look at the model. What division does it show?

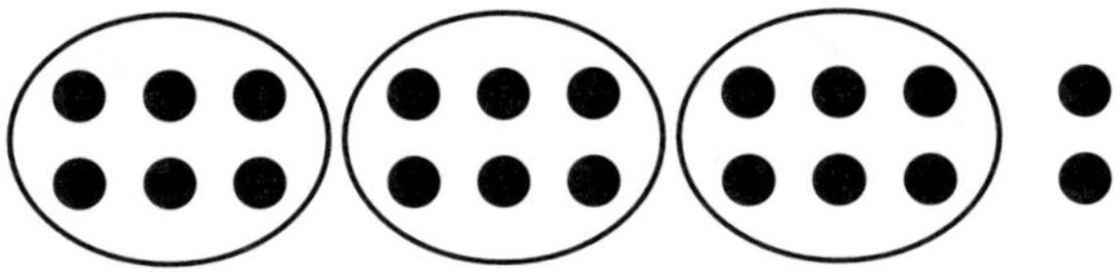

A $6 \div 3 = 2$

B $6 \div 4 \longrightarrow 1$ r2

C $18 \div 3 = 6$

D $20 \div 3 \longrightarrow 6$ r2

20. Sylvia plans to place 617 stamps in an album. Each page of the album holds 5 stamps. She uses division to find out how many full pages she will have. In what place is the first digit of the quotient?

A thousands

B hundreds

C tens

D ones

21. A crayon factory packs 5 crayons in a sample pack. The factory gives sample packs away to visitors under 12. How many sample packs can be made with 2,500 crayons?

A 5

B 50

C 500

D 5000

GO ON

22. A store gave away 1,932 calendars in 7 days. They gave away the same number of calendars each day. How many calendars did the store give away each day?

A 266

B 276

C 281

D 776

23. Vanna uses thank-you notes that come in packs of 8. She has to write 29 thank-you notes. How many packs of thank-you notes should she buy?

A 3

B $3\frac{5}{8}$

C 4

D 5

24. Chad bought 8 dozen note pads for his office. The note pads were divided equally into 6 boxes. How many note pads are in each box?

A 4

B 9

C 12

D 16

25. Liz estimated 228 ÷ 7 to be between 30 and 40. Which basic facts did she use to help her estimate?

A 14 ÷ 7 and 21 ÷ 7

B 21 ÷ 7 and 28 ÷ 7

C 30 ÷ 5 and 40 ÷ 5

D 40 ÷ 5 and 45 ÷ 5

GO ON

Name ________________________________

26. A kennel is moving 160 dogs to a new facility. Each dog has its own crate. Each truck holds 9 dogs in their crates. What is the number of trucks needed to carry the dogs in their crates?

Show your work.

Answer ________ trucks

27. There are 48 people waiting for a fishing tour. Each boat holds 12 people. Rodney used the work below to find the number of boats needed. Explain how Rodney's work can be used to find the number of boats needed. How many boats are needed?

$$\begin{array}{r} 12\overline{)48} \\ -12 \\ \hline 36 \\ -12 \\ \hline 24 \\ -12 \\ \hline 12 \\ -12 \\ \hline 0 \end{array}$$

Answer ____

____

____

GO ON

Name ______________________________

28. Ethan needs to divide these base-ten blocks into 3 equal groups. What is the model that can be used to show how many are in each group?

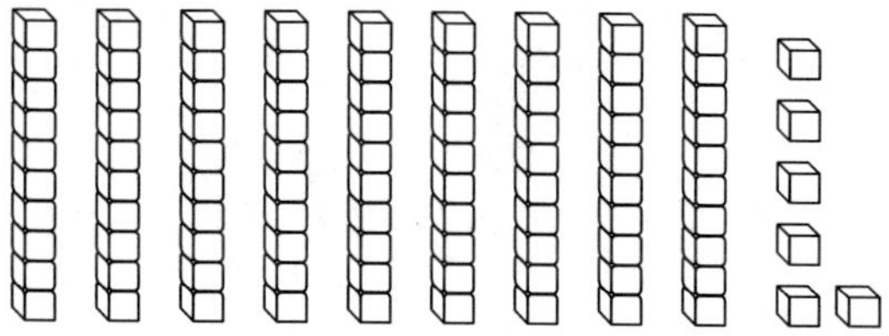

Answer

29. A science show brings along everything it needs for a show in big trucks.

PART A

The science show sets up chairs in rows with 8 seats in each row. How many rows will need to be set up if 456 people are expected to attend the show?

Answer ________ rows

PART B

The lizards in the show eat about 250 crickets per week. About how many crickets do the lizards eat each day? Explain.

Answer ______________________________

____

____

____

STOP

Name ______________________________

Choose the correct answer.

1. Josh works in a balloon store. He will put 45 balloons into bunches. He must use the same number of balloons in each bunch. The number of balloons in each bunch must be greater than 1 and less than 10. How many balloons could be in each bunch?

A 4

B 5

C 6

D 8

2. Cecilia was skip counting with a friend on the school bus. Cecilia started to count by 7s. She said 7, 14, 21, 28, and 35. What number will she say next?

A 36

B 40

C 42

D 49

3. Ms. Chan is Dwight's math teacher. During class, she asked if the number 6 is a prime number or a composite number. How should Dwight answer Ms. Chan's question?

A 6 is prime.

B 6 is composite.

C 6 is neither prime nor composite.

D 6 is both prime and composite.

4. Marissa is decorating her room. She arranges 63 picture tiles on a wall in the shape of a rectangle. Which is **not** a possible arrangement of the picture tiles?

A 7 rows of 9 tiles

B 21 rows of 3 tiles

C 22 rows of 6 tiles

D 63 rows of 1 tile

5. In a math game, Rob reads four statements about the number 51. He has to pick the true statement to win the game. Which statement should Rob choose?

A 51 is divisible by 2.

B 51 is divisible by 3.

C 51 is divisible by 5.

D 51 is a prime number.

GO ON

6. Janice spent $54 to buy some pairs of pants. Each pair of pants cost the same whole-dollar amount. How many pairs of pants could she have bought?

A 3

B 4

C 5

D 7

7. Ms. Ayers wrote a bonus problem on the board. If Jason correctly answers, he will get extra computer time. The problem is to write a statement that correctly relates the numbers 5 and 10. Which should Jason write?

A 5 is a multiple of 10.

B 10 is a factor of 5.

C 10 is a common multiple of 5 and 10.

D 15 is a common multiple of 5 and 10.

8. Caitlin's teacher wrote a row of numbers with a pattern.

75, 68, 70, 63, 65, 58, 60, . . .

What is the rule for the pattern?

A *add* 2, *subtract* 7

B *add* 5, *subtract* 2

C *subtract* 7, *add* 2

D *subtract* 2, *add* 5

9. Miles has a train collection with 36 engines, 72 boxcars, and 18 cabooses. He wants to arrange the train cars in equal rows, with only one type of train car in each row. How many can he put in each row?

A 1 or 18

B 1, 2, 9, or 18

C 1, 2, 3, 6, 9, or 18

D 1, 2, 3, 4, 6, 8, 9, 12, 18, 24, 36, or 72

GO ON

10. Marta uses 1 piece of paper and 1 piece of ribbon to make kites. The paper comes in packs of 3 pieces, and the ribbon comes in packs of 4 pieces. What is the least number of kites Marta can make without any supplies left over?

A 10

B 11

C 12

D 14

11. Jenn will use 18 connecting cubes to make a model of a park. The model will be in the shape of a rectangle and will have a height of one cube. In how many different ways can Jenn make the model of the park?

A 1

B 2

C 3

D 17

12. Aidan makes 12 bracelets on Monday. He makes 20 bracelets on Tuesday. He continues to make 8 more bracelets each day from Wednesday through Friday. How many bracelets does Aidan make on Friday?

A 20 **C** 44

B 32 **D** 56

13. Elina had 10 tiles to arrange in a rectangular design. She drew a model of the rectangles she could make with the 10 tiles.

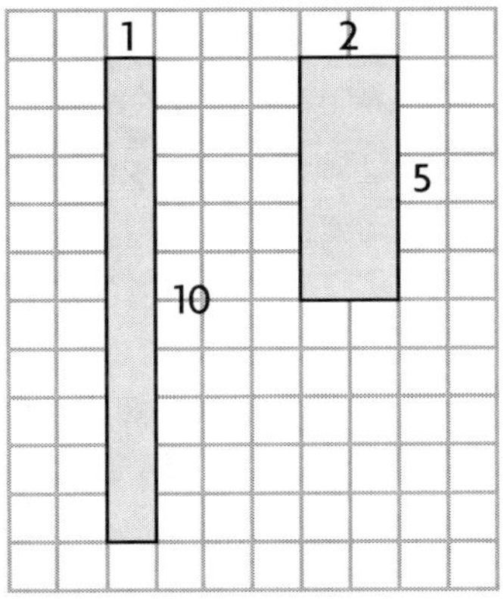

What can Elina conclude about the number 10 from her model?

A 10 is a prime number.

B 10 is a composite number.

C 10 is neither prime nor composite.

D 10 is both prime and composite.

GO ON

14. Marie made 3 dozen cookies. She needs to put them into equal groups so that the number of groups is at least 4 but less than 10. What are all the possible equal-size groups she can make with all the cookies?

A 4, 6, or 9 groups

B 4 or 6 groups

C 4 or 9 groups

D 4, 6, or 8 groups

15. Jorge gives an equal number of marbles to 6 friends. Which could be the total number of marbles he gave to his friends?

A 15

B 33

C 56

D 60

16. Petra and Peter were playing a game. Petra was counting by 9s. Peter was counting by 4s. They paced the counting so that they would say the first common number together. What is the first number that both said together?

A 16

B 36

C 45

D 64

17. Sean helps his coach at the end of the game. He needs to put away 24 baseballs. He puts the same number of baseballs into each box. Which list shows how many baseballs could be in each box?

A 1, 3, 4, or 7

B 2, 4, 6, or 7

C 2, 6, 8, or 10

D 3, 4, 6, or 8

GO ON

Name ____________________

18. Kendall has 45 dolphin stickers, 15 shark stickers, and 20 whale stickers. She wants to put an equal number of stickers into bags, with only one type of sticker in each bag. How many stickers can Kendall put in each bag?

A 1

B 1 or 5

C 1, 3, 4, or 5

D 1, 2, 3, 4, 5, 9, 10, 15, 20, or 45

19. Julie used chalk to write numbers on the chairs for field day. She marked the number 4 on the first chair. Her rule was *add* 5. What numbers did she write on the first six chairs?

A 4, 8, 13, 18, 23, 28

B 4, 9, 14, 19, 24, 29

C 5, 9, 13, 17, 21, 25

D 9, 14, 19, 24, 29, 34

20. Maria tells her friend that she is learning about prime numbers in math class. Her friend writes down 4 numbers and asks Maria to choose the prime number. Which number should Maria choose?

A 21

B 23

C 25

D 27

21. Lee and 4 friends want to play marbles. Lee has 40 marbles to share among them. All players must have the same number of marbles to start the game. How many marbles should each player get?

A 5

B 8

C 10

D 20

GO ON

Name ______________________________

22. Beverly was skip counting while jumping rope. She started to count by 9s. She said 9, 18, 27, 36, 45, and 54. What number will she say next?

A 59

B 61

C 63

D 67

23. Miles has a train collection with 36 engines, 72 boxcars, and 18 cabooses. He wants to arrange all the train cars in rows of equal number with only one type of train car in each row. Which of the following would Miles **not** be able to put in each row?

A 2 train cars

B 3 train cars

C 9 train cars

D 11 train cars

24. Emily wants to make a rectangular model with a height of one connecting cube. She wants to make the model in exactly 2 different ways. How many connecting cubes could Emily use to make the model in **only** two ways?

A 6

B 12

C 16

D 18

25. Ben and Irie made a secret code. They wrote some numbers of the code so they could remember the pattern.

7, 12, 10, 15, 13, 18, 16, 21

What should the next number be?

A 18

B 19

C 23

D 26

GO ON

Name ________________________________

26. The library is designing a book display with 20 fiction books, 28 biographies, and 40 nonfiction books. Each shelf will have only one type of book on it. List the common factors of 20, 28, and 40. What is the highest number of books that can be put on each shelf?

Show your work.

Answer __________ books

27. Gus wrote the following riddle: I am a number between 30 and 60. My ones digit is three less than my tens digit. I am a prime number. What number does Gus's riddle describe? Explain.

Answer ____

____

____

____

____

____

____

GO ON

28. Use the rule to write the first five terms of the pattern. What is the fifth term?

Rule: Add 8, subtract 4   First term: 13

Show your work.

Answer __________

29. The number of books featured at the local library is shown in the table.

Books	
Type of Book	**Number of Books**
mystery	32
novel	16
nonfiction	12

PART A

The local library is hosting a book fair in August that features the mystery books. All authors discuss the same number of mystery books and each will discuss **more than** 1 mystery book. How many authors could be featured in the show?

Answer ____________ authors

PART B

The library wants to display all the books on shelves in rows. Each row has the same number of books and the same type of books. How many books could be in each row?

Answer ____________ books

STOP

Name ____________________

Choose the correct answer.

1. Henry has two same-size rectangles divided into the same number of equal parts. One rectangle has $\frac{2}{5}$ of the parts shaded, and the other has $\frac{1}{2}$ of the parts shaded. Into how many parts could each rectangle be divided?

A 2

B 5

C 7

D 10

2. Martin fills an aquarium $\frac{4}{5}$ full of water. Which fraction is equivalent to $\frac{4}{5}$?

A $\frac{5}{6}$

B $\frac{6}{7}$

C $\frac{7}{10}$

D $\frac{8}{10}$

3. In the school band, $\frac{6}{24}$ of the members play the trumpet. In simplest form, what fraction of the band plays the trumpet?

A $\frac{1}{3}$

B $\frac{1}{4}$

C $\frac{2}{8}$

D $\frac{3}{12}$

4. Bill used $\frac{3}{8}$ cup of raisins and $\frac{2}{3}$ cup of banana chips to make a snack. His brother asked if he used more raisins or banana chips in his snack. Which statement correctly compares the fractions?

A $\frac{3}{8} > \frac{2}{3}$

B $\frac{2}{3} < \frac{3}{8}$

C $\frac{2}{3} > \frac{3}{8}$

D $\frac{2}{3} = \frac{3}{8}$

GO ON

5. Jing is helping the kindergarten teacher put together bags of crayons. Each bag has 4 crayons, and $\frac{1}{4}$ of the crayons in each bag are green. What fraction of the crayons in 3 bags is green?

A $\frac{3}{12}$

B $\frac{3}{4}$

C $\frac{4}{3}$

D $\frac{12}{3}$

6. Allie worked for $\frac{1}{2}$ hour on Saturday and for $\frac{3}{4}$ hour on Sunday. Which number is a common denominator for $\frac{1}{2}$ and $\frac{3}{4}$?

A 1

B 4

C 6

D 10

7. Nicolette needs $\frac{1}{3}$ yard of fabric. Which fraction is equivalent to $\frac{1}{3}$?

A $\frac{1}{9}$

B $\frac{5}{15}$

C $\frac{2}{3}$

D $\frac{15}{5}$

8. Jamal made a list of fractions and asked Will to find the fraction written in simplest form. Which fraction should Will choose?

A $\frac{1}{8}$

B $\frac{3}{9}$

C $\frac{9}{18}$

D $\frac{6}{10}$

GO ON

9. Ann runs $\frac{2}{5}$ mile. Kim runs $\frac{1}{2}$ mile. Which statement is **true**?

A $\frac{2}{5} > \frac{1}{2}$

B $\frac{1}{2} > \frac{2}{5}$

C $\frac{1}{2} = \frac{2}{5}$

D $\frac{1}{2} < \frac{2}{5}$

10. Jenna's recipe calls for $\frac{1}{2}$ cup of flour. She only has a $\frac{1}{4}$ cup measure. Which equivalent fraction shows the amount of flour she can use for the recipe?

A $\frac{1}{4}$

B $\frac{2}{6}$

C $\frac{2}{4}$

D $\frac{3}{4}$

11. Michael works at an apple orchard that sells bags of apples. He puts 12 apples in each bag, and $\frac{5}{12}$ of the apples are Cortland apples. If Michael makes 4 bags of apples, how many Cortland apples does he need?

A 5

B 12

C 20

D 48

12. In Jason's homeroom, $\frac{8}{30}$ of the students like soccer best. In simplest form, what fraction of the students in Jason's homeroom like soccer best?

A $\frac{3}{10}$

B $\frac{2}{7}$

C $\frac{4}{15}$

D $\frac{1}{4}$

GO ON

13. Swati is putting 5 stickers in each gift bag. Each bag has 2 silver stickers. If Swati makes 5 gift bags, what fraction of the stickers will be silver?

A $\frac{10}{25}$

B $\frac{2}{3}$

C $\frac{5}{2}$

D $\frac{25}{10}$

14. Brad uses $\frac{3}{4}$ cup of milk and $\frac{1}{8}$ cup of yogurt in a recipe. Which statement correctly compares the amounts of milk and yogurt Brad uses in the recipe?

A $\frac{3}{4} < \frac{1}{8}$

B $\frac{3}{4} > \frac{1}{8}$

C $\frac{3}{4} = \frac{1}{8}$

D $\frac{1}{8} > \frac{3}{4}$

15. Jeff is making muffins. He combines $\frac{1}{6}$ cup milk, $\frac{1}{8}$ cup raisins, and $\frac{1}{3}$ cup butter. Which list shows the order of the ingredients from the **least** amount to the **greatest** amount?

A $\frac{1}{8}, \frac{1}{6}, \frac{1}{3}$

B $\frac{1}{8}, \frac{1}{3}, \frac{1}{6}$

C $\frac{1}{3}, \frac{1}{6}, \frac{1}{8}$

D $\frac{1}{3}, \frac{1}{8}, \frac{1}{6}$

16. Al has his grandmother's recipe for making mixed nuts.

$\frac{3}{4}$ cup pecans
$\frac{1}{2}$ cup almonds
$\frac{2}{12}$ cup peanuts
$\frac{7}{8}$ cup walnuts

Which statement about the recipe is **true**?

A The amount of almonds is greater than the amount of pecans.

B The amount of walnuts is greater than the amount of almonds.

C The amount of pecans is equal to the amount of peanuts.

D The amount of pecans is less than the amount of peanuts.

GO ON

17. Edgar, Jack, and Katie walked around Woodbury Lake. Edgar walked $\frac{3}{5}$ of the distance in an hour. Jack walked $\frac{3}{4}$ of the distance in an hour. Ellen walked $\frac{6}{8}$ of the distance in an hour. Which inequality correctly compares the distances walked by each person?

A $\frac{3}{4} > \frac{3}{5}$

B $\frac{3}{4} < \frac{6}{8}$

C $\frac{6}{8} < \frac{3}{4}$

D $\frac{6}{8} < \frac{3}{5}$

18. Jamal helps in the library. He put away $\frac{1}{3}$ of the books on Monday and $\frac{5}{6}$ of the books on Tuesday. Which number is a common denominator for $\frac{1}{3}$ and $\frac{5}{6}$?

A 2

B 3

C 6

D 9

19. Mr. Adams is driving Betsy, Ed, and Beth home from the mall. Betsy lives $\frac{1}{4}$ mile from the mall, Ed lives $\frac{2}{3}$ mile from the mall, and Beth lives $\frac{1}{2}$ mile from the mall. Which shows the fractions in order from **least** to **greatest**?

A $\frac{1}{4}, \frac{2}{3}, \frac{1}{2}$

B $\frac{1}{4}, \frac{1}{2}, \frac{2}{3}$

C $\frac{1}{2}, \frac{1}{4}, \frac{2}{3}$

D $\frac{2}{3}, \frac{1}{2}, \frac{1}{4}$

20. Cassie bought $\frac{3}{8}$ pound of raisins and $\frac{1}{4}$ pound of dried cranberries for a snack. Which inequality or equation correctly compares the amounts of raisins and dried cranberries?

A $\frac{3}{8} < \frac{1}{4}$

B $\frac{1}{4} > \frac{3}{8}$

C $\frac{1}{4} = \frac{3}{8}$

D $\frac{3}{8} > \frac{1}{4}$

GO ON

Name ______________________

21. Ben walked $\frac{3}{4}$ mile to Ming's house. Sarah walked the same distance to Ming's house. Which shows how far Sarah walked?

A $\frac{3}{8}$ mile

B $\frac{3}{6}$ mile

C $\frac{6}{8}$ mile

D $\frac{12}{8}$ miles

22. Suzanne arranges flowers in vases at her restaurant. Each vase has 12 flowers, and $\frac{2}{3}$ of the flowers are yellow. What other fraction can represent the part of the flowers that are yellow?

A $\frac{8}{12}$

B $\frac{6}{12}$

C $\frac{4}{9}$

D $\frac{1}{3}$

23. Carmen has completed $\frac{1}{2}$ of her math homework. Billy has completed $\frac{7}{12}$ of the same assignment. Which statement correctly compares the fractions?

A $\frac{1}{2} > \frac{7}{12}$

B $\frac{1}{2} < \frac{7}{12}$

C $\frac{7}{12} = \frac{1}{2}$

D $\frac{7}{12} < \frac{1}{2}$

24. Miguel walked $\frac{1}{2}$ mile to the library and then $\frac{3}{5}$ mile to the post office. How can he write $\frac{1}{2}$ and $\frac{3}{5}$ as a pair of fractions with a common denominator?

A $\frac{1}{10}$ and $\frac{3}{10}$

B $\frac{3}{6}$ and $\frac{3}{5}$

C $\frac{2}{4}$ and $\frac{15}{25}$

D $\frac{5}{10}$ and $\frac{6}{10}$

25. James and Ella biked around Eagle Lake. James biked $\frac{3}{10}$ of the distance in an hour. Ella biked $\frac{4}{8}$ of the distance in an hour. Which statement correctly compares the fractions?

A $\frac{3}{10} > \frac{4}{8}$

B $\frac{4}{8} = \frac{3}{10}$

C $\frac{3}{10} < \frac{4}{8}$

D $\frac{4}{8} < \frac{3}{10}$

GO ON

Name ____________________________

26. Georgina has $\frac{3}{8}$ yard of blue fabric and $\frac{1}{4}$ yard of red fabric. Does she have the same amount of blue and red fabric? Shade the model to show your work.

blue fabric:

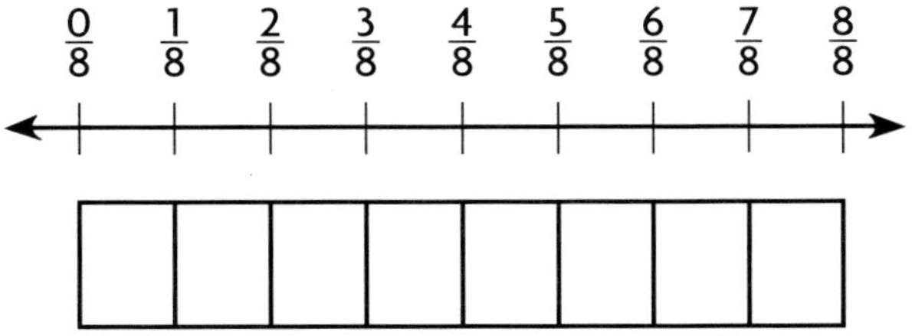

red fabric:

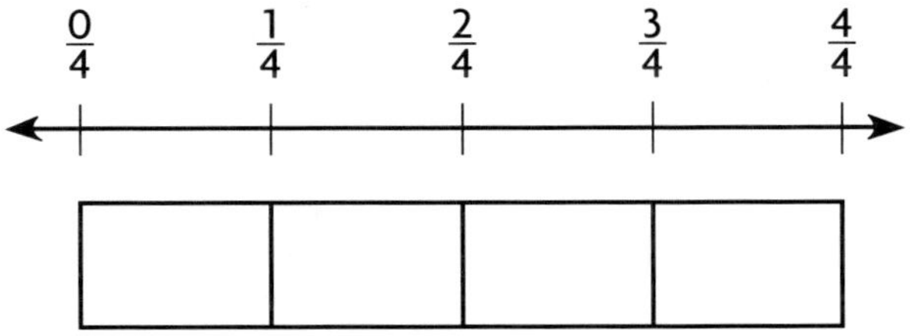

Answer ________

27. The table shows the distances of some places in town from the school.

Distance from School	
Place	**Distance**
Library	$\frac{3}{5}$ mile
Post Office	$\frac{1}{2}$ mile
Park	$\frac{3}{4}$ mile
Town Hall	$\frac{8}{10}$ mile

What is the order of the places by their distance from school, from least to greatest?

Show your work.

Answer ______________________________

GO ON

Name ________________________________

28. Craig is tiling the floor of his bathroom. He wants $\frac{1}{4}$ of the tiles to be brown. What other fractions can represent the part of the tiles that will be brown? Shade the models to show your work.

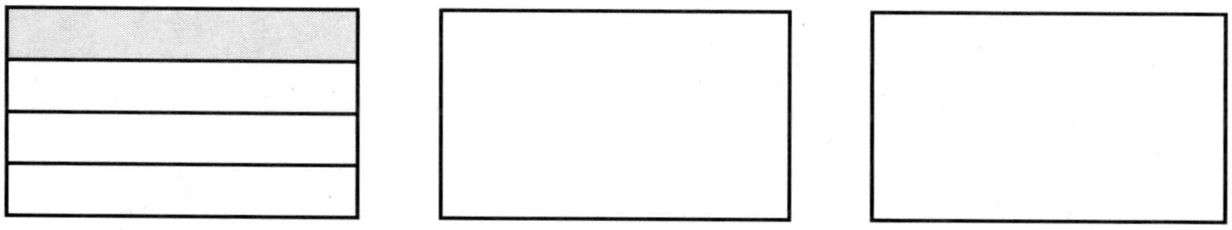

$\frac{1}{4}$ $\qquad$ $\frac{\square}{20}$ $\qquad$ $\frac{\square}{\square}$

Answer ____________________

29. Naomi swims $\frac{2}{5}$ mile. Chloe swims $\frac{5}{8}$ mile. They want to compare how far they each swam using the benchmark $\frac{1}{2}$.

PART A

How do Naomi's distance and Chloe's distance compare to the benchmark?

Show your work.

Answer ________________________________

____

PART B

Did Naomi swim farther than, the same distance as, or less than Chloe?

Answer ____________________

STOP

Name ______________________________

Choose the correct answer.

1. Ben uses $\frac{3}{12}$ pound of strawberries and $\frac{2}{12}$ pound of blueberries to make jam.

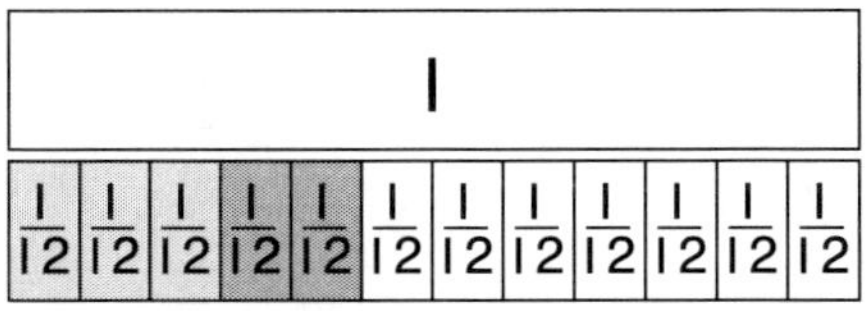

How many pounds of berries does Ben use to make jam?

A $\frac{1}{12}$ pound

B $\frac{5}{24}$ pound

C $\frac{5}{12}$ pound

D $\frac{1}{2}$ pound

2. Dillon's dad sells golf balls online. He sells $\frac{4}{5}$ of the golf balls. Which is equivalent to $\frac{4}{5}$?

A $\frac{1}{5} + \frac{1}{5} + \frac{1}{5}$

B $\frac{1}{5} + \frac{1}{5} + \frac{2}{5}$

C $\frac{2}{5} + \frac{2}{5} + \frac{1}{5}$

D $\frac{1}{5} + \frac{1}{5} + \frac{1}{5} + \frac{1}{5} + \frac{1}{5}$

3. Ellen sewed $\frac{5}{8}$ yard of fringe on her scarf. Ling sewed $\frac{2}{8}$ yard of fringe on her scarf.

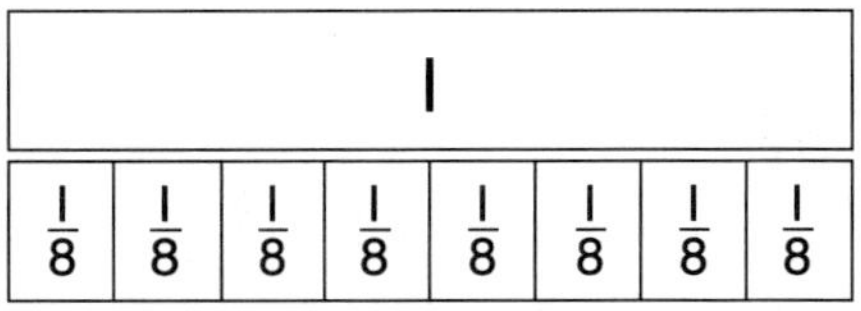

How much **more** fringe did Ellen sew on her scarf than Ling?

A $\frac{1}{8}$ yard

B $\frac{2}{8}$ yard

C $\frac{3}{8}$ yard

D $\frac{7}{8}$ yard

4. Wanda rode her bike $\frac{21}{10}$ miles. Which mixed number shows how far Wanda rode her bike?

A $1\frac{1}{10}$ miles

B $1\frac{2}{10}$ miles

C $2\frac{1}{10}$ miles

D $2\frac{10}{10}$ miles

GO ON

Name ________________________________

5. Ryan's collection is $\frac{3}{6}$ football cards and $\frac{2}{6}$ basketball cards. What part of Ryan's card collection is **not** football or basketball cards?

A $\frac{1}{6}$

B $\frac{5}{12}$

C $\frac{5}{6}$

D 1

6. Nick had $3\frac{1}{4}$ bottles of water for his wrestling practice. When he finished practice, he had $1\frac{2}{4}$ bottles of water left. How much water did he use during practice?

A $1\frac{3}{4}$

B 2

C $2\frac{1}{4}$

D $2\frac{2}{4}$

7. Mindi planted beans in $\frac{4}{10}$ of her garden and peas in $\frac{5}{10}$ of her garden. What fraction of the garden has beans or peas?

A $\frac{1}{10}$

B $\frac{9}{20}$

C $\frac{8}{10}$

D $\frac{9}{10}$

8. Which equation shows the use of the Commutative Property?

A $\frac{3}{5} + \left(\frac{2}{5} + \frac{1}{5}\right) = \left(\frac{3}{5} + \frac{2}{5}\right) + \frac{1}{5}$

B $3\frac{1}{5} + \left(5 + 1\frac{3}{5}\right) = 3\frac{1}{5} + \left(1\frac{3}{5} + 5\right)$

C $\left(4\frac{1}{8} + \frac{1}{8}\right) + 2\frac{7}{8} = 4\frac{1}{8} + \left(\frac{1}{8} + 2\frac{7}{8}\right)$

D $1\frac{4}{10} + 1\frac{1}{10} + 3\frac{6}{10} = 1\frac{4}{10} + \left(1\frac{1}{10} + 3\frac{6}{10}\right)$

GO ON

Name ______________________________

9. Sue used $2\frac{3}{8}$ cups of walnuts and $1\frac{2}{8}$ cups of almonds to make a nut mix. How many **more** cups of walnuts than almonds did Sue use?

A $\frac{1}{8}$ cup

B $1\frac{1}{8}$ cups

C $3\frac{1}{8}$ cups

D $3\frac{5}{8}$ cups

10. Santos used a unit fraction to describe how much of his book he has read. Which fraction could Santos have used?

A $\frac{9}{10}$

B $\frac{4}{5}$

C $\frac{5}{8}$

D $\frac{1}{3}$

11. Ted needs $\frac{5}{8}$ yard of denim and $\frac{2}{8}$ yard of canvas to make a tote bag. How much fabric does Ted need in all?

A $\frac{1}{8}$ yard

B $\frac{3}{8}$ yard

C $\frac{7}{16}$ yard

D $\frac{7}{8}$ yard

12. Ilene is making smoothies. The recipe calls for $1\frac{1}{4}$ cups of strawberries. How many cups of strawberries, written as a fraction greater than one, are used in the recipe?

A $\frac{4}{5}$ cup

B $\frac{5}{4}$ cups

C $\frac{6}{4}$ cups

D $\frac{11}{4}$ cups

13. Royce walks $\frac{3}{4}$ mile to school and $\frac{3}{4}$ mile home each day. In how many days will he have walked 3 miles?

A 2

B 4

C 6

D 8

GO ON

14. Betsy brought $\frac{6}{12}$ pound of trail mix on a camping trip. She ate $\frac{4}{12}$ pound of the trail mix. How much trail mix is left?

A $\frac{1}{12}$ pound

B $\frac{2}{12}$ pound

C $\frac{3}{12}$ pound

D $\frac{10}{12}$ pound

15. Paige hiked $5\frac{5}{6}$ miles. Xavier hiked $2\frac{1}{6}$ miles. How many **fewer** miles did Xavier hike than Paige?

A $2\frac{1}{6}$ miles

B $3\frac{2}{6}$ miles

C $3\frac{4}{6}$ miles

D 8 miles

16. Harrison ate $\frac{3}{12}$ of a pizza. Miles ate $\frac{5}{12}$ of the same pizza. How much **more** of the pizza did Miles eat than Harrison?

A $\frac{2}{12}$

B $\frac{2}{6}$

C $\frac{6}{12}$

D $\frac{8}{12}$

17. A quarter is $\frac{1}{4}$ of a dollar. Victor has 32 quarters. How much money does he have?

A $8

B $7

C $6

D $5

GO ON

Name ______________________________

18. Lee's birthday is in $3\frac{4}{7}$ weeks. Which shows the number of weeks until Lee's birthday written as a fraction greater than one?

A $\frac{34}{7}$

B $\frac{25}{7}$

C $\frac{24}{7}$

D $\frac{14}{7}$

19. Ryan has two pet hamsters. One hamster weighs $\frac{3}{10}$ pound. The other hamster weighs $\frac{4}{10}$ pound. What is the difference in the weights of Ryan's hamsters?

A $\frac{1}{10}$ pound

B $\frac{2}{10}$ pound

C $\frac{7}{10}$ pound

D $\frac{12}{10}$ pounds

20. Aidan is making cinnamon apples. He needs $4\frac{1}{4}$ teaspoons of cinnamon. He needs $2\frac{3}{4}$ teaspoons of nutmeg. How much **more** cinnamon than nutmeg will he need?

A $1\frac{2}{4}$ teaspoons

B $1\frac{3}{4}$ teaspoons

C 2 teaspoons

D $2\frac{1}{4}$ teaspoons

21. Which fraction is equivalent to $5\frac{1}{6}$?

A $\frac{12}{5}$

B $\frac{17}{6}$

C $\frac{31}{5}$

D $\frac{31}{6}$

GO ON

22. Which equation shows the Associative Property being used correctly?

A $\frac{3}{5} + \left(\frac{2}{5} + \frac{1}{5}\right) = \left(\frac{3}{5} + \frac{2}{5}\right) + \frac{1}{5}$

B $\left(4\frac{1}{8} + \frac{1}{8}\right) + 2\frac{7}{8} = 4\frac{2}{8} + 2\frac{7}{8}$

C $3\frac{1}{5} + \left(5 + 1\frac{3}{5}\right) = 3\frac{1}{5} + \left(1\frac{3}{5} + 5\right)$

D $\left(1\frac{4}{10} + 1\frac{1}{10}\right) + 3\frac{6}{10} = 2\frac{5}{10} + 3\frac{6}{10}$

23. What is the sum of $6\frac{7}{10}$ and $2\frac{1}{10}$?

A $4\frac{8}{10}$

B $8\frac{6}{10}$

C $8\frac{8}{10}$

D $9\frac{1}{10}$

24. Sue is selling pet treats at the school fair. She made $\frac{3}{8}$ of the treats for dogs and $\frac{2}{8}$ of the treats for cats. The rest of the treats are for other types of pets. What fraction of the pet treats is for cats and dogs?

A $\frac{1}{8}$

B $\frac{2}{8}$

C $\frac{5}{8}$

D $\frac{7}{8}$

25. In a survey, $\frac{3}{6}$ of the students chose summer as their favorite season and $\frac{1}{6}$ chose winter. What fraction of the students surveyed chose summer or winter?

A $\frac{1}{6}$

B $\frac{2}{6}$

C $\frac{4}{12}$

D $\frac{4}{6}$

GO ON

26. In a survey, $\frac{5}{10}$ of the students chose a dog and $\frac{1}{10}$ chose a fish as their favorite pet. What fraction shows the students that chose a dog or a fish as their favorite pet? Shade the model to show your answer.

1									
$\frac{1}{10}$	$\frac{1}{10}$	$\frac{1}{10}$	$\frac{1}{10}$	$\frac{1}{10}$	$\frac{1}{10}$	$\frac{1}{10}$	$\frac{1}{10}$	$\frac{1}{10}$	$\frac{1}{10}$

Answer ____

27. Lucy needs to find $\frac{3}{9} + \frac{2}{9}$. Her work shows $\frac{3}{9} + \frac{2}{9} = \frac{5}{18}$. Is she correct? Why or why not? If she isn't correct, what is the correct answer?

Show your work.

Answer ______________________________________

____

____

GO ON

Name ______________________________

28. What is $\frac{6}{10} + \frac{2}{10}$?

Show your work.

Answer ____

29. The school carnival is divided into sections. The dunk tanks are in $\frac{1}{10}$ of the carnival. Games are in $\frac{4}{10}$ of the carnival. Student exhibits are in $\frac{5}{10}$ of the carnival.

PART A

What fraction of the carnival is dunk tanks and games? Shade the model to show your answer.

1									
$\frac{1}{10}$	$\frac{1}{10}$	$\frac{1}{10}$	$\frac{1}{10}$	$\frac{1}{10}$	$\frac{1}{10}$	$\frac{1}{10}$	$\frac{1}{10}$	$\frac{1}{10}$	$\frac{1}{10}$

Answer ____

PART B

How much **greater** is the part of the carnival with student exhibits than that with games?

Show your work.

Answer ____

STOP

Name ______________________________

Choose the correct answer.

1. Craig used repeated addition to show $3 \times \frac{3}{5}$. Which shows an expression Craig could write?

A $\frac{1}{5} + \frac{1}{5} + \frac{1}{5}$

B $\frac{3}{5} + \frac{3}{5} + \frac{3}{5}$

C $\frac{3}{15} + \frac{3}{15} + \frac{3}{15}$

D $3 + \frac{1}{5} + \frac{1}{5} + \frac{1}{5}$

2. Rudi is comparing shark lengths. She read that a sandbar shark is $4\frac{1}{2}$ feet long. A thresher shark is 3 times as long as that. Use the bar model. How long is a thresher shark?

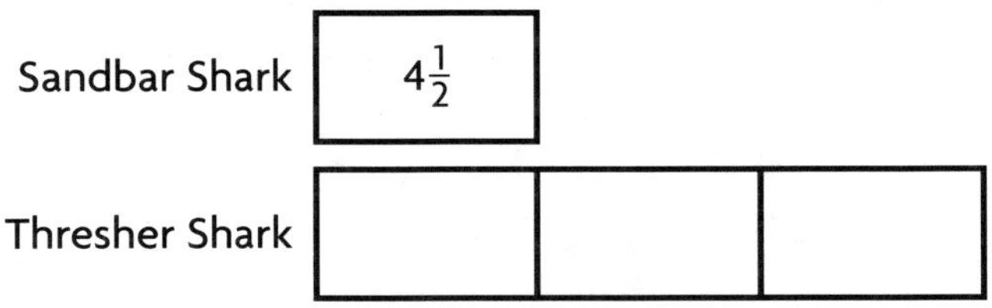

A $7\frac{1}{2}$ feet

B 12 feet

C $13\frac{1}{2}$ feet

D 15 feet

3. Aaron made a list of some multiples of $\frac{1}{8}$. Which could be Aaron's list?

A $\frac{1}{8}, \frac{2}{8}, \frac{3}{8}, \frac{4}{8}, \frac{5}{8}$

B $\frac{1}{8}, \frac{1}{16}, \frac{1}{24}, \frac{1}{32}, \frac{1}{40}$

C $\frac{1}{8}, \frac{2}{9}, \frac{3}{10}, \frac{4}{11}, \frac{5}{12}$

D 1, 2, 3, 4, 5

4. Amanda is building a fence. She needs a pole to measure $4\frac{5}{6}$ feet from the ground. How can she write $4\frac{5}{6}$ feet as a fraction?

A $\frac{30}{6}$ feet

B $\frac{29}{6}$ feet

C $\frac{24}{6}$ feet

D $\frac{20}{6}$ feet

GO ON

Name ______________________________

5. Phil made a number line showing multiples of $\frac{3}{6}$.

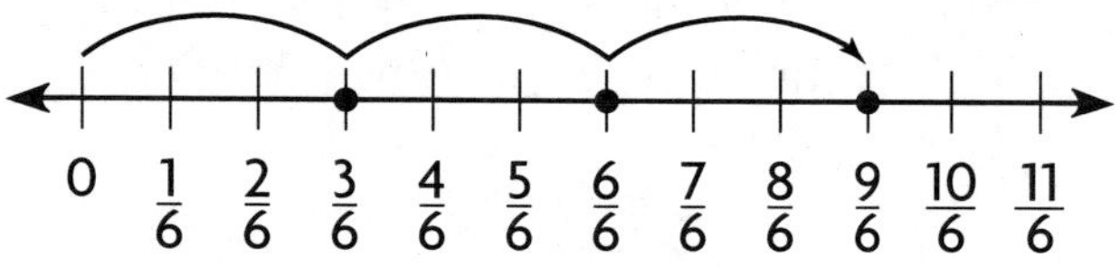

Which fraction on the number line shows the product of $2 \times \frac{3}{6}$?

A $\frac{2}{6}$

B $\frac{3}{6}$

C $\frac{6}{6}$

D $\frac{9}{6}$

6. Trevor weighed $6\frac{3}{8}$ pounds when he was born. By age 5, he weighed 5 times as much. If p stands for pounds, which equation could you use to find Trevor's weight at age 5?

A $p = (5 \times 6) + \frac{3}{8}$

B $p = 5 + 6\frac{3}{8}$

C $p = 5 \times 6\frac{3}{8}$

D $p = \left(5 \times \frac{3}{8}\right) + 6$

7. Gwen listed the multiples of $\frac{3}{10}$. Which is **not** a multiple of $\frac{3}{10}$?

A $\frac{8}{10}$

B $\frac{9}{10}$

C $\frac{15}{10}$

D $\frac{30}{10}$

8. One day, the outdoor temperature increased by $\frac{5}{10}$ degree every hour for 6 hours. How much did the temperature increase by the end of 6 hours?

A $\frac{11}{10}$ degrees

B $\frac{15}{10}$ degrees

C $\frac{20}{10}$ degrees

D $\frac{30}{10}$ degrees

GO ON

Name ____

9. Sandi buys some fabric to make a quilt. She needs $\frac{1}{5}$ yard of each type of fabric. She has 9 different types of fabrics to make her design. Sandi writes the following equation. What number goes in the box to make the statement true?

$$\frac{9}{5} = \square \times \frac{1}{5}$$

A 4

B 5

C 8

D 9

10. Malak solved a problem that had an answer of $\frac{33}{5}$. How can Malak write $\frac{33}{5}$ as a mixed number?

A $6\frac{3}{5}$

B $5\frac{3}{5}$

C $4\frac{3}{5}$

D $\frac{33}{5}$

11. Look at the fraction number line. What fraction goes directly below the 2?

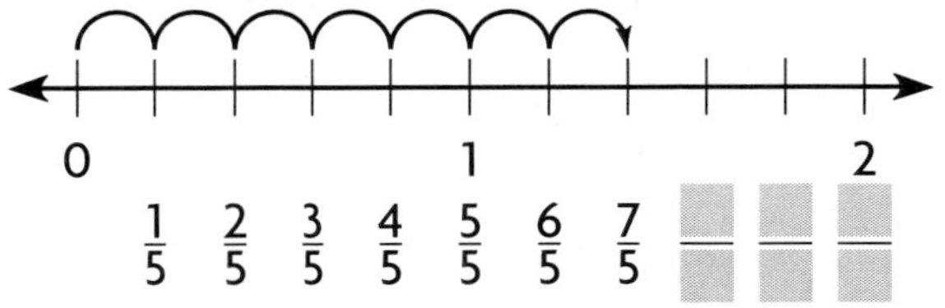

A $\frac{3}{10}$

B $\frac{3}{5}$

C $\frac{8}{5}$

D $\frac{10}{5}$

12. The train takes $1\frac{1}{2}$ hours to get from Arno to Bentley. The train takes 5 times as long as that to get from Arno to Valdez. How long is the train ride from Arno to Valdez?

A 15 hours

B $7\frac{1}{2}$ hours

C 7 hours

D $6\frac{1}{2}$ hours

13. Alice walks $\frac{6}{10}$ mile every day. How far does Alice walk in 5 days?

A $\frac{15}{10}$ miles

B $\frac{30}{10}$ miles

C 10 miles

D 15 miles

GO ON

14. Hanna is baking 3 batches of health bars. She needs $1\frac{2}{3}$ cups of carob chips for each batch of bars. What is the correct number of cups Hannah needs for 3 batches of bars?

A $3\frac{2}{3}$

B 5

C $5\frac{1}{3}$

D 6

15. Oleg made a fraction number line to help him multiply $4 \times \frac{2}{5}$.

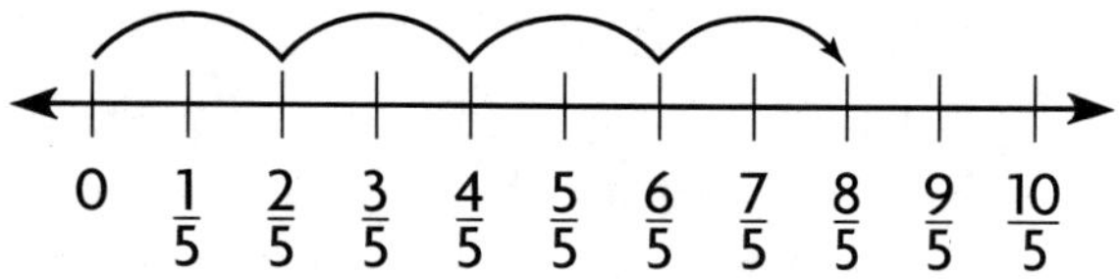

Which shows $4 \times \frac{2}{5}$ written as the product of a whole number and a unit fraction?

A $4 \times \frac{1}{5}$

B $4 \times \frac{2}{5}$

C $8 \times \frac{1}{5}$

D $8 \times \frac{1}{4}$

16. Carrie spends $1\frac{1}{4}$ hours practicing the piano 3 times a week. How much time does Carrie spend practicing the piano in one week?

A $4\frac{1}{4}$ hours

B 4 hours

C $3\frac{3}{4}$ hours

D $3\frac{1}{4}$ hours

17. Mrs. Tokala uses $\frac{9}{10}$ of a can of coffee beans each week. How many cans of coffee beans does Mrs. Tokala use in 6 weeks?

A $\frac{54}{60}$

B $\frac{54}{10}$

C $\frac{65}{10}$

D $\frac{69}{10}$

GO ON

18. Sarah is making 4 batches of granola bars. She adds $\frac{7}{8}$ cup peanuts to each batch. Her measuring cup holds $\frac{1}{8}$ cup. How many times must Sarah measure $\frac{1}{8}$ cup of peanuts to have enough for the granola bars?

A 32

B 28

C 24

D 21

19. Tom made macaroni salad. He used $1\frac{1}{8}$ cups of mayonnaise. He used 9 times as much macaroni. How many cups of macaroni did Tom use?

A 81 cups

B 18 cups

C $10\frac{1}{8}$ cups

D $9\frac{2}{3}$ cups

20. Malik wants to give $\frac{3}{5}$ of his balloons to his friends. How can $\frac{3}{5}$ be written as the product of a whole number and a unit fraction?

A 3×5

B $1 \times \frac{3}{5}$

C $3 \times \frac{1}{5}$

D $1 \times \frac{1}{5} + 1 \times \frac{1}{5} + 1 \times \frac{1}{5}$

21. What are three multiples of $\frac{4}{5}$?

A $\frac{6}{5}, \frac{8}{5}, \frac{10}{5}$

B $\frac{8}{5}, \frac{12}{5}, \frac{16}{5}$

C $\frac{4}{10}, \frac{4}{15}, \frac{4}{20}$

D $\frac{8}{10}, \frac{12}{15}, \frac{16}{20}$

GO ON

22. Violet used $1\frac{3}{4}$ gallons of paint to paint her kitchen. She needed 4 times as much paint to paint her living room and bedrooms. How much paint did Violet use for the living room and bedrooms?

A 28 gallons

B $8\frac{1}{4}$ gallons

C 7 gallons

D $5\frac{3}{4}$ gallons

23. Tara has softball practice Tuesday, Wednesday, Thursday, and Sunday. Each practice is $1\frac{1}{3}$ hours. How many hours will Tara practice this week?

A $1\frac{2}{3}$

B $4\frac{2}{3}$

C 5

D $5\frac{1}{3}$

24. What are the next four multiples of $\frac{1}{7}$?

A $\frac{1}{7}, \frac{2}{7}, \frac{3}{7}, \frac{4}{7}$

B $\frac{2}{7}, \frac{3}{7}, \frac{4}{7}, \frac{5}{7}$

C $\frac{2}{7}, \frac{4}{7}, \frac{6}{7}, \frac{8}{7}$

D $\frac{1}{8}, \frac{1}{9}, \frac{1}{10}, \frac{1}{11}$

25. Mr. Tuyen uses $\frac{5}{8}$ of a tank of gas each week to drive to and from his job. How many tanks of gas does Mr. Tuyen use in 5 weeks?

A $\frac{40}{8}$

B $\frac{25}{8}$

C $\frac{10}{8}$

D $\frac{5}{40}$

GO ON

Name ____________________

26. What is the correct product for the equation?

$4 \times \frac{3}{8} = \blacksquare$

Show your work.

Answer ________

27. What are the first four multiples of $\frac{1}{3}$?

Show your work.

Answer ________

28. Mrs. McGlashan is making paint for her class. She needs $\frac{3}{4}$ cup of warm water for each student's paint. Mrs. McGlashan has a 1-cup measure that has no other markings. Can she make paint for 8 students using only the 1-cup measure?

Show your work.

Answer _____

GO ON

29. Maddie is making a batch of popcorn balls. She uses $1\frac{1}{4}$ cups of raisins. She uses 5 times as much popcorn as she does raisins.

PART A

Draw a model to show the problem.

PART B

Use your model to write an equation. Then solve the equation to find the amount of popcorn Maddie needs.

Show your work.

Answer ________ cups

STOP

Name ______________________________

Choose the correct answer.

1. Which fraction is equivalent to 0.2?

A $\frac{2}{100}$

B $\frac{2}{10}$

C $\frac{2}{0}$

D $\frac{1}{2}$

2. Cora paid $\frac{65}{100}$ of a dollar to buy a postcard from Grand Canyon National Park in Arizona. What is $\frac{65}{100}$ written as a decimal in terms of dollars?

A 0.65

B 6.05

C 6.5

D 65

3. Which is the decimal shown by the model?

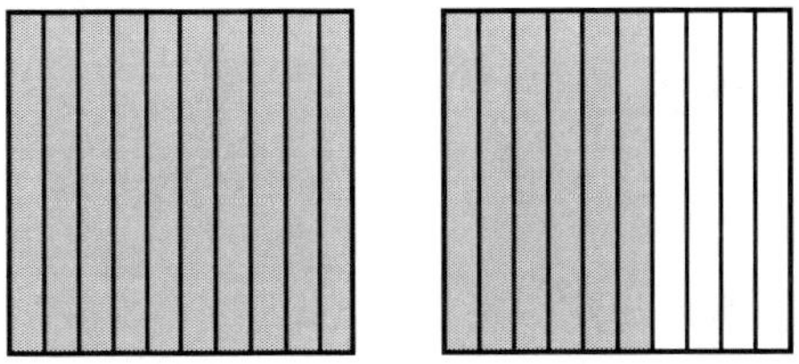

A 16.0

B 10.6

C 6.1

D 1.6

4. Randy is comparing statistics from a baseball tournament. Which decimal is **less** than 0.4?

A 0.38

B 0.40

C 0.44

D 1.04

GO ON

5. Winona has 4 quarters and 1 nickel. Which does **not** represent the value of 4 quarters and 1 nickel?

A \$1.05

B $1\frac{5}{100}$ dollars

C 1.05 dollars

D $1\frac{5}{10}$ dollars

6. The weight of a diamond is measured in carats. Mrs. Wang has a diamond that weighs $1\frac{5}{100}$ carats. Which decimal is equivalent to $1\frac{5}{100}$?

A 0.15

B 1.05

C 1.5

D 1.50

7. What is the sum of $\frac{4}{10}$ and $\frac{55}{100}$?

A $\frac{59}{110}$

B $\frac{59}{100}$

C $\frac{95}{100}$

D $\frac{95}{10}$

8. Haroun is comparing decimals. Which statement is **true**?

A $0.5 > 0.53$

B $0.35 = 0.53$

C $0.35 < 0.3$

D $0.35 > 0.3$

GO ON

Name ______________________________

9. Denny ran $2\frac{1}{10}$ miles along a marathon route. What is this distance written as a decimal?

A 0.21 mile

B 2.01 miles

C 2.1 miles

D 21.0 miles

10. Ryan sold a jigsaw puzzle at a yard sale for three dollars and five cents. Which decimal names this money amount in terms of dollars?

A 3.50

B 3.05

C 0.55

D 0.05

11. What is the sum of $\frac{2}{10}$ and $\frac{20}{100}$?

A $\frac{21}{100}$

B $\frac{4}{10}$

C $\frac{22}{110}$

D $\frac{40}{200}$

12. The U.S. Senate in Washington, D.C., has 100 elected members who make laws for the United States. Last year, 30 senators ran for reelection. Which decimal is equivalent to $\frac{30}{100}$?

A 3.100

B 0.3

C 0.03

D 0.003

13. Chaz needs $4.77 for new batteries. He has $2.80. How much **more** money does he need?

A $1.97

B $2.10

C $2.17

D $7.57

GO ON

14. Which decimal is equivalent to $1\frac{68}{100}$?

A 0.68

B 1.68

C 68.1

D 168.0

15. Brianna filled seven tenths of the pages in her stamp album. Which of the following is **not** equivalent to seven tenths?

A $\frac{7}{10}$

B 0.7

C 0.70

D 0.07

16. The point on the number line shows how far Emily needs to ride her bike to Piper's house. Which decimal correctly names the distance Emily needs to ride her bike?

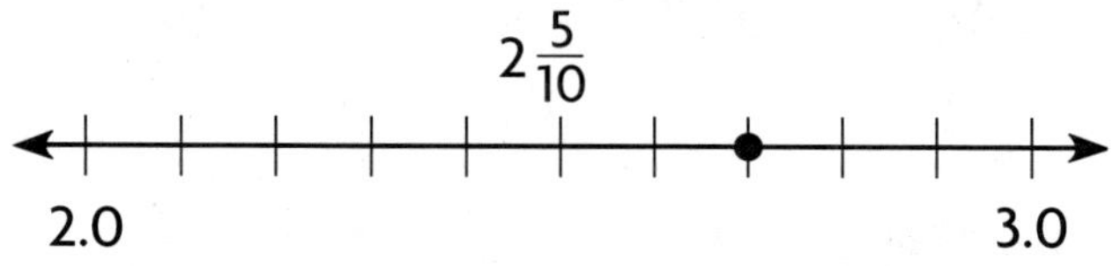

A 2.06

B 2.07

C 2.6

D 2.7

17. Which decimal is **less than** 3.81 but **greater than** 3.0?

A 2.99

B 3.2

C 3.85

D 3.9

GO ON

18. Jack drew a model to represent the number of miles from his home to the park. Which decimal matches the model?

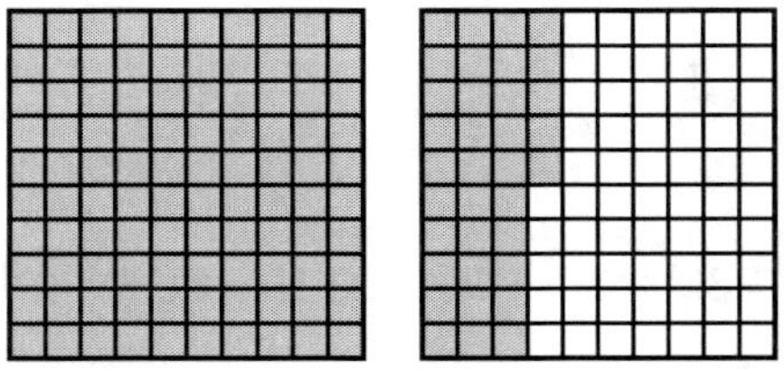

A 0.35

B 1.35

C 1.45

D 10.35

19. Maya and three of her friends have three quarters and one nickel to spend. If Maya and her friends share the money equally, how much will each person get?

A $0.20

B $0.25

C $0.40

D $0.80

20. Maria has these coins in her wallet.

What is Maria's total amount as a fraction in terms of a dollar?

A $\frac{59}{100}$

B $\frac{75}{100}$

C $\frac{134}{100}$

D $\frac{100}{59}$

21. What is the sum of $\frac{2}{10} + \frac{30}{100}$?

A $\frac{5}{100}$

B $\frac{32}{100}$

C $\frac{5}{10}$

D $\frac{50}{10}$

GO ON

22. Anna paid $\frac{98}{100}$ of a dollar to buy a used comic book. Which shows $\frac{98}{100}$ as a money amount?

A \$0.098

B \$0.98

C \$1.98

D \$9.8

23. Patty, Helene, and Mira share \$0.96 that they found in an old wallet. How much money does each girl get?

A \$0.32

B \$0.36

C \$0.38

D \$0.48

24. Charlie's model shows the number of hours he exercised yesterday.

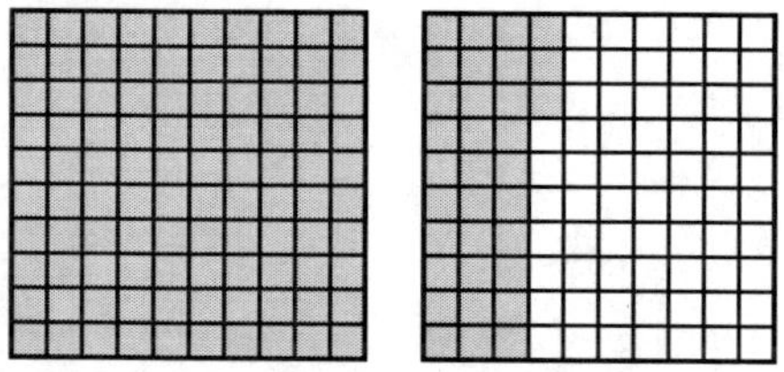

Which decimal and mixed number does the model show?

A 1.03, $1\frac{3}{100}$

B 1.3, $1\frac{3}{10}$

C 1.33, $1\frac{33}{100}$

D 3.3, $3\frac{3}{10}$

25. Matthew walks $\frac{4}{10}$ mile to Zack's house. Which fraction is equivalent to $\frac{4}{10}$?

A $\frac{4}{100}$

B $\frac{40}{100}$

C $\frac{44}{100}$

D $\frac{40}{10}$

GO ON

Name ______________________________

26. Gene lives 0.6 mile from school. Kate lives 0.51 mile from school. Who lives closer to the school? Use fractions to find the answer.

Show your work.

Answer ____

27. After selling lemonade and cookies, Vivian and her brother Gil had 7 one-dollar bills, 8 quarters, and 6 dimes. What is the total amount of money that Vivian and Gil earned?

Show your work.

Answer ____

GO ON

28. Julian is building a birdhouse. The house is $\frac{21}{100}$ meter high without the roof. The roof is $\frac{3}{10}$ meter high. What is the height of the birdhouse with the roof?

Show your work.

Answer ____ meter

29. Jen is making pancakes. A recipe calls for $\frac{4}{10}$ kilogram flour and $\frac{12}{100}$ kilogram sugar.

PART A

If Jen measures correctly and combines the two amounts, how much flour and sugar will she have?

Show your work.

Answer ___ kilogram

PART B

How can you write your answer as a decimal?

Answer ____ kilogram

STOP

Name ______________________________

Choose the correct answer.

1. Claire painted the following figures. Which figure has **more** than one line of symmetry?

A 

B 

C 

D 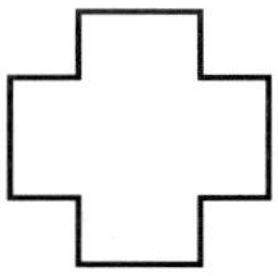

2. Given Figure A below, which angle is the right angle?

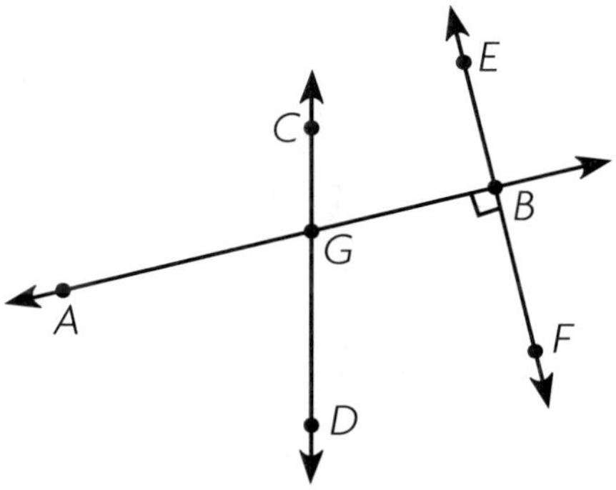

Figure *A*

A $\angle DGB$

B $\angle AGD$

C $\angle GBF$

D $\angle CGB$

3. The patio in Keith's backyard is in the shape of a rhombus. Which figure could be the shape of Keith's patio?

A 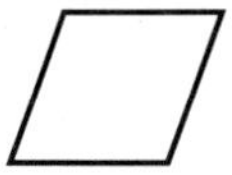

B 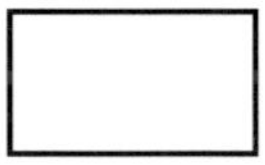

C 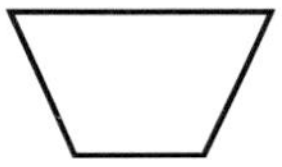

D 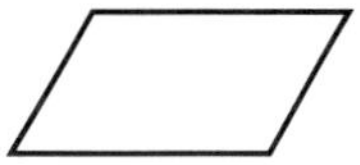

4. Which image has only one line of symmetry?

A 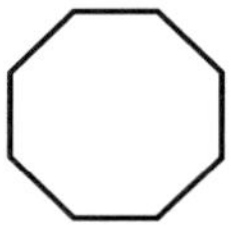

B 

C **S**

D 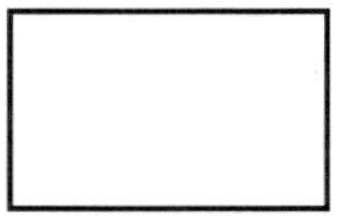

GO ON

Name ____________________________________

5. Which of the following terms **best** describes this figure?

A line segment

B line

C ray

D angle

6. A sign is in the shape of an acute triangle. Which of the following could be the shape of the sign?

A
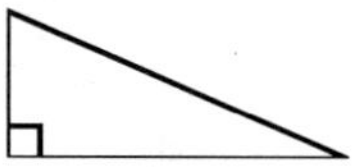

B
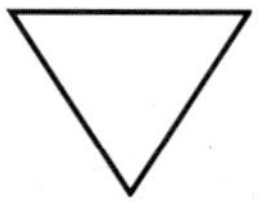

C

D
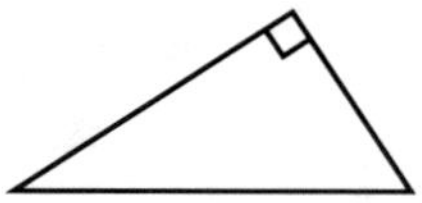

7. Gloria painted this pattern on the wall of her bedroom.

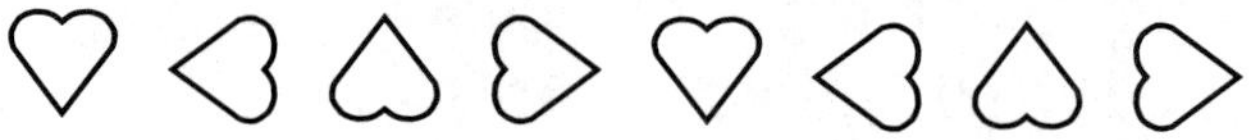

Which could be the next three figures in this pattern?

A

B

C

D

8. Mrs. Perkin's class was folding paper for an art project. Which shape can be folded on the line to show symmetry?

A
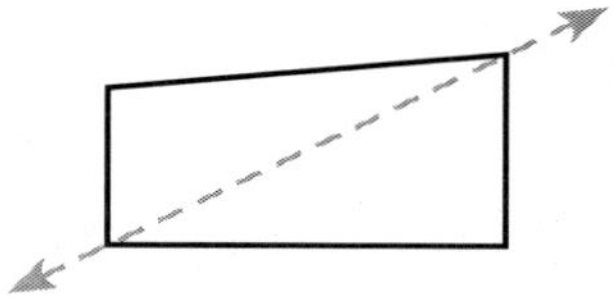

B
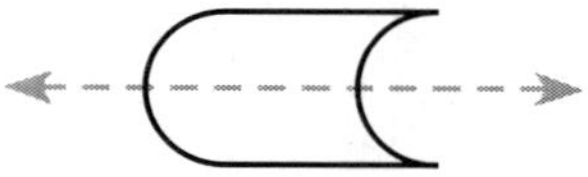

C
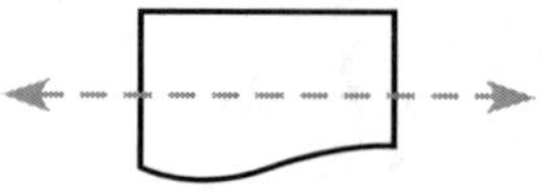

D
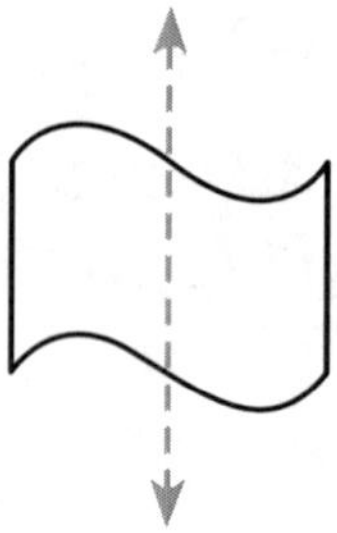

GO ON

Name ______________________________

9. Which set of angles identifies an obtuse triangle?

A right, acute, acute

B obtuse, right, acute

C acute, obtuse, acute

D acute, acute, acute

10. Joe drew a figure. Which two sides of the figure are perpendicular?

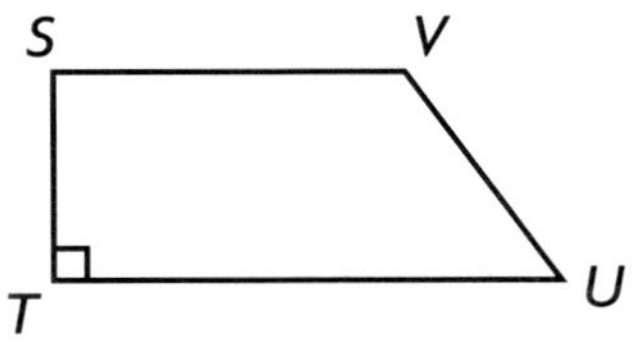

A $\overline{TU}$ and $\overline{UV}$

B $\overline{ST}$ and $\overline{VU}$

C $\overline{SV}$ and $\overline{TU}$

D $\overline{TU}$ and $\overline{ST}$

11. Vinny draws an angle like the one shown for the first letter of his name.

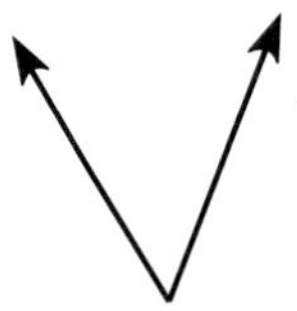

What kind of angle does Vinny draw?

A right angle

B straight angle

C acute angle

D obtuse angle

12. How many acute angles does an acute triangle have?

A 0

B 1

C 2

D 3

13. Jim's vegetable garden looks like this quadrilateral.

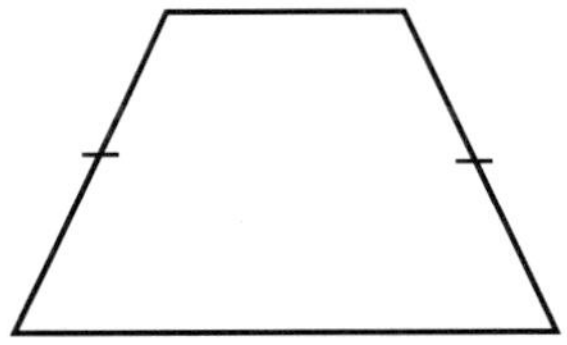

What type of quadrilateral is it?

A trapezoid

B square

C rhombus

D rectangle

GO ON

14. Logan draws a map of his neighborhood.

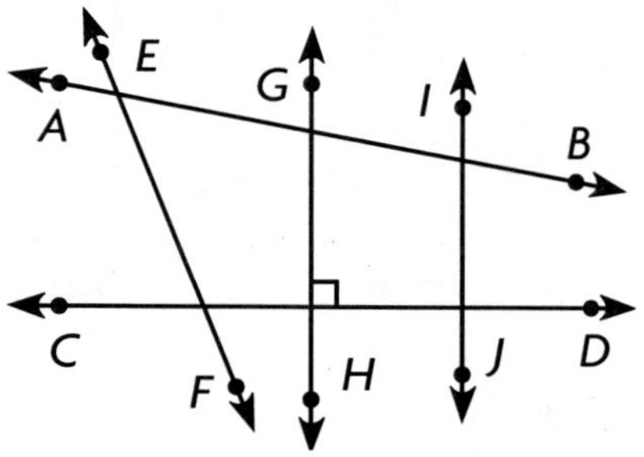

Which line appears to be parallel to $\overleftrightarrow{GH}$?

A $\overleftrightarrow{AB}$

B $\overleftrightarrow{CD}$

C $\overleftrightarrow{EF}$

D $\overleftrightarrow{IJ}$

15. Rosie drew a triangle and its line of symmetry. Which could be the figure that Rosie drew?

A

B

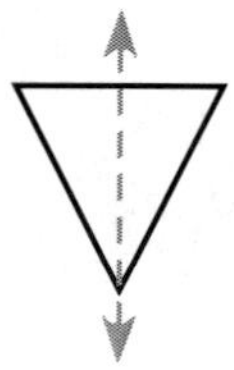

C

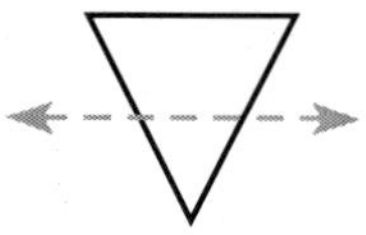

D

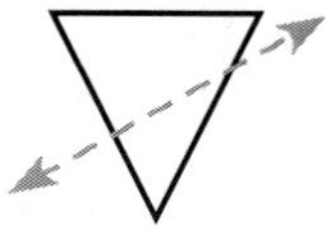

16. Mrs. Becker drew an obtuse angle on the chalkboard. Which of the following could be the angle she drew?

A

B

C

D

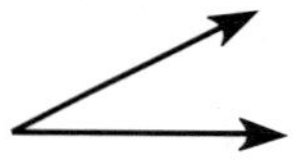

17. The figure shown has 8 sides of equal length.

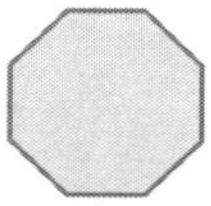

How many lines of symmetry does the figure appear to have?

A 2

B 4

C 8

D 10

GO ON

18. Martha used counters to make this pattern.

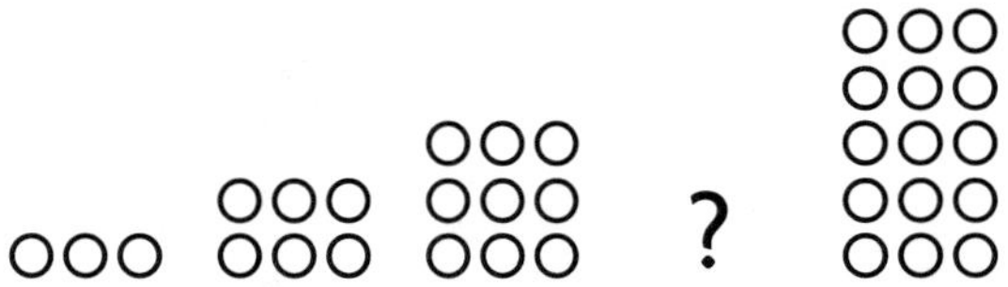

How many counters should she use in the missing figure?

A 10

B 12

C 14

D 18

19. Which of the letters does **not** have line symmetry?

HEFT

A H

B E

C F

D T

20. How many lines of symmetry does the figure have?

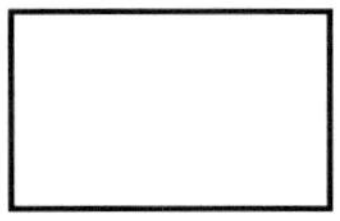

A 0

B 1

C 2

D 4

21. Which of the letters does **not** have line symmetry?

CATS

A C

B A

C T

D S

GO ON

Name ______________________________

22. Which is **not** a way to name this angle?

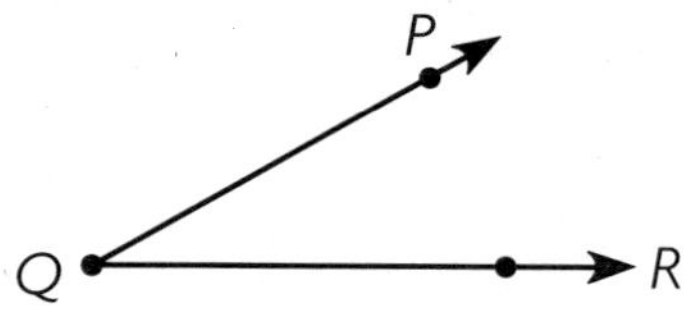

A $\angle PQR$

B $\angle PRQ$

C $\angle Q$

D $\angle RQP$

23. Virginia and Susan are discussing properties of lines during math class. Which statement **best** describes intersecting lines?

A They cross each other at one point.

B They always form obtuse angles.

C They only form right angles.

D They never cross each other.

24. Alison has a sticker in the shape of a quadrilateral that has 2 pairs of parallel sides and no right angles. Which could be the shape of the sticker?

A trapezoid

B parallelogram

C rectangle

D square

25. Addison made this pattern by shading squares.

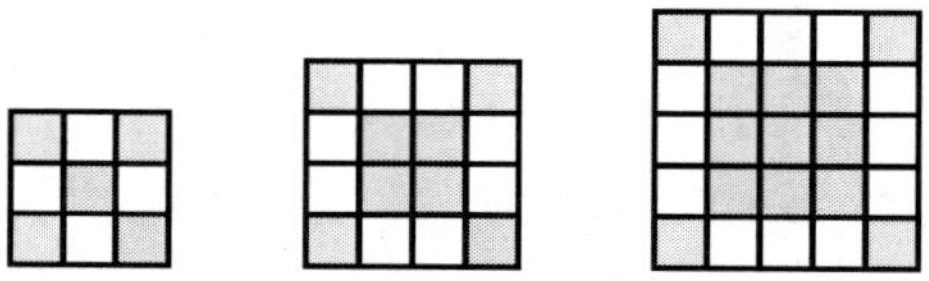

If Addison continues this pattern, how many squares should she shade in the next figure?

A 13

B 20

C 25

D 36

GO ON

Name ____________________

26. Compare the 2 quadrilaterals. Tell how they are alike, and identify three ways that they are different.

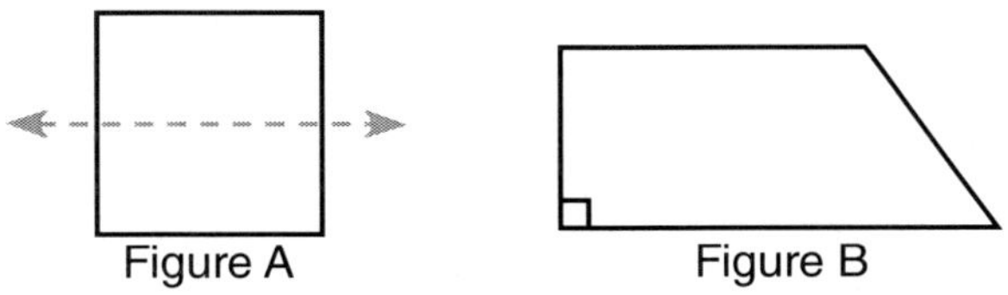

Answer

Alike: ____________________

Different: ____________________

27. Debbie leaves for her trip to San Diego on the 13th day of February. Since February is the 2nd month, Debbie wrote the date as shown. Debbie says all the numbers she wrote have at least one line of symmetry. Is she correct? Draw the lines of symmetry where possible.

Answer ____

GO ON

Name ________________________________

28. Leah says both figures are squares. Do you agree with Leah? Support your answer.

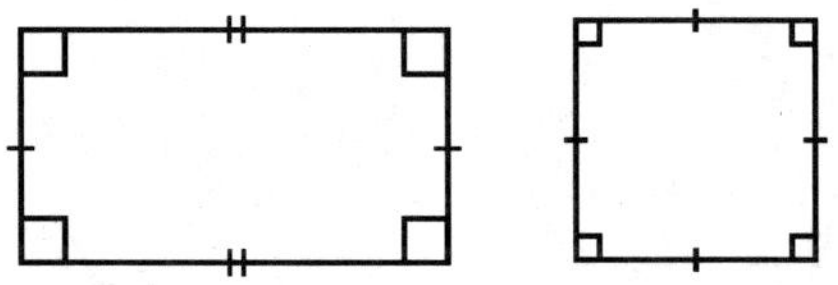

Figure 1 Figure 2

Answer ________________________________

____

____

____

29. Jon drew the pattern shown.

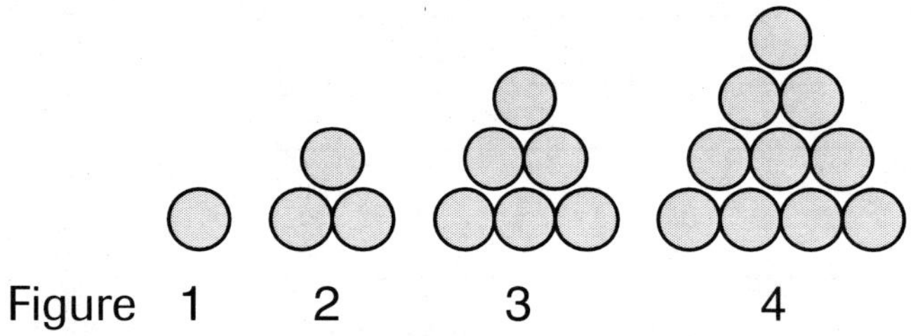

PART A

Write a rule using numbers to find the number of circles in any figure in the pattern.

Answer ________________________________

____

PART B

Draw Figure 5.

STOP

Name ______________________________

Choose the correct answer.

1. How many degrees are in an angle that turns through $\frac{3}{4}$ of a circle?

A 90°

B 180°

C 270°

D 360°

2. Use a protractor. What is the measure of $\angle JKL$?

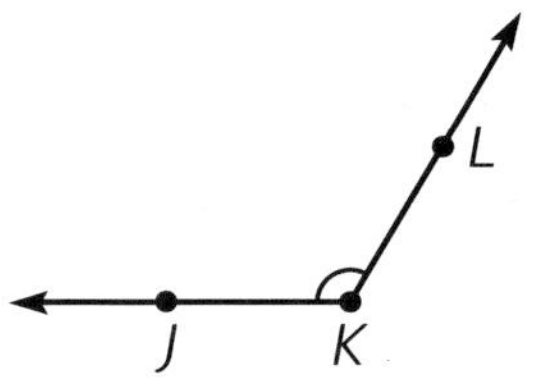

A 50°

B 60°

C 110°

D 120°

Use the diagram for 3–4.

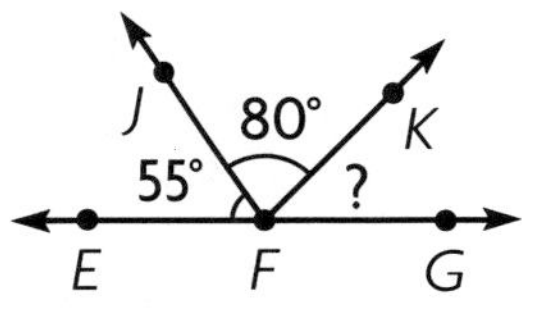

3. Which equation can you use to find the $m\angle KFG$?

A $55° + 80° = \square$

B $180° - 80° = \square$

C $180° - 55° = \square$

D $180° - (55° + 80°) = \square$

4. Which is an obtuse angle?

A $\angle EFJ$

B $\angle GFK$

C $\angle JFG$

D $\angle JFK$

GO ON

Name ______________________________

Use the diagram for 5–6.

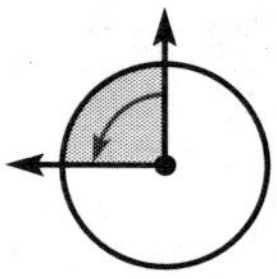

5. The angle in the figure represents what fraction of a turn?

A $\frac{1}{4}$

B $\frac{1}{3}$

C $\frac{1}{2}$

D $\frac{3}{4}$

6. Which equation shows how to find the angle measure of the part of the circle without the arrow?

A $180^\circ - 90^\circ = \square$

B $360^\circ - 90^\circ = \square$

C $360^\circ - 180^\circ = \square$

D $360^\circ - 270^\circ = \square$

7. Use a protractor. Which angle measures 30°?

A 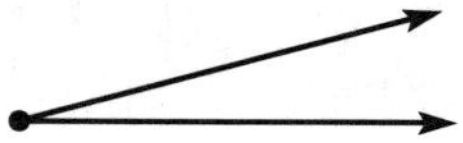

B 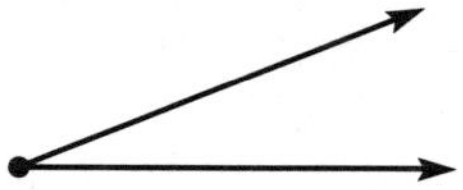

C 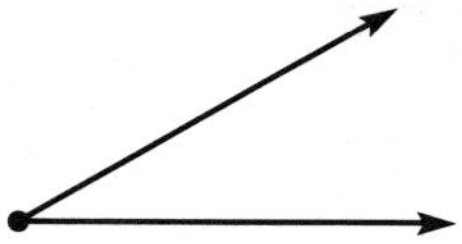

D 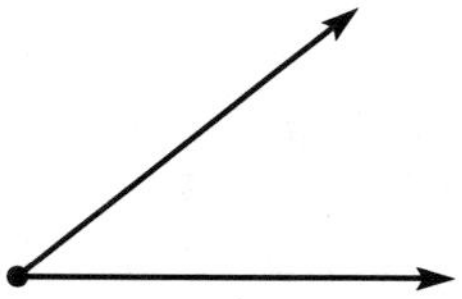

8. Alejandro drew an acute angle. Which could be the measure of the angle he drew?

A 60°

B 90°

C 120°

D 180°

GO ON

9. Marla has a piece of felt that is $\frac{1}{3}$ of a large circle. She cuts the piece of felt in half from the center point of the circle. What is the angle measure of each part?

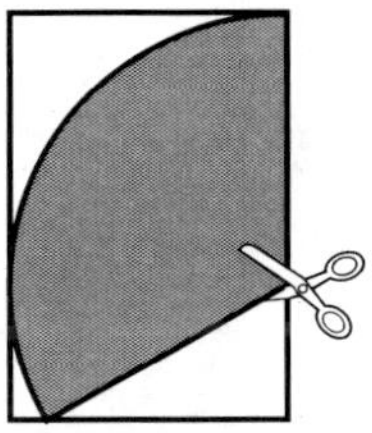

A 30°

B 60°

C 90°

D 120°

10. Use a protractor. What is the measure of the angle formed by the hands of the clock?

A 360°

B 180°

C 90°

D 45°

11. Using the figure below, what is the measurement of the unknown angle?

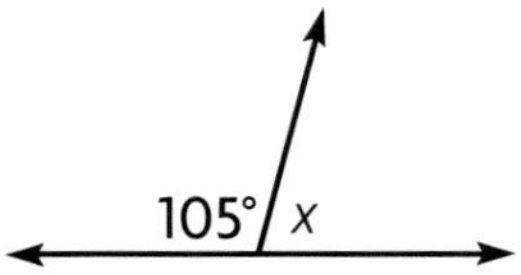

A 180°

B 75°

C 60°

D 15°

12. Two angles form a straight angle. One angle measures 107°. What is the measure of the other angle?

A 253°

B 83°

C 73°

D 17°

GO ON

Name ________________________________

13. Which two angle measures form a right angle?

A 90° and 90°

B 45° and 90°

C 60° and 45°

D 60° and 30°

14. An angle measures 51°. Through what fraction of a circle does the angle turn?

A $\frac{1}{51}$

B $\frac{51}{90}$

C $\frac{51}{180}$

D $\frac{51}{360}$

15. What term **best** describes the angle formed by the hands of the clock?

A acute

B obtuse

C right

D straight

16. What is the measure of the unknown angle in the figure?

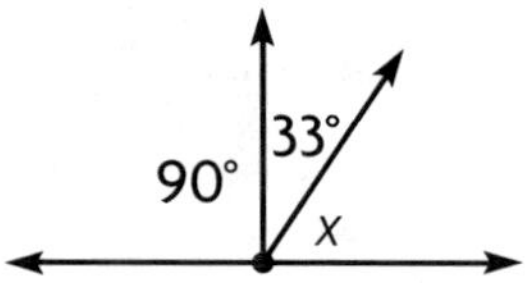

A 47°

B 57°

C 90°

D 123°

17. Two angles form a straight angle. One angle measures 30°. What is the measure of the other angle?

A 60°

B 120°

C 150°

D 180°

GO ON

Use the diagram for 18–19.

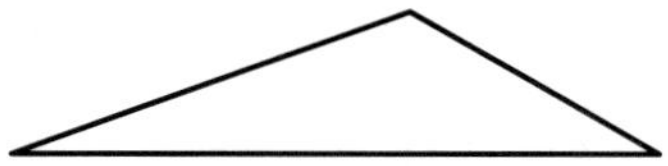

18. Which term **best** describes the triangle?

A acute

B obtuse

C right

D straight

19. Use a protractor. What is the measure of the greatest angle in the triangle?

A 150°

B 130°

C 50°

D 20°

20. Look at the figure. In degrees, what is the angle measure of the shaded part?

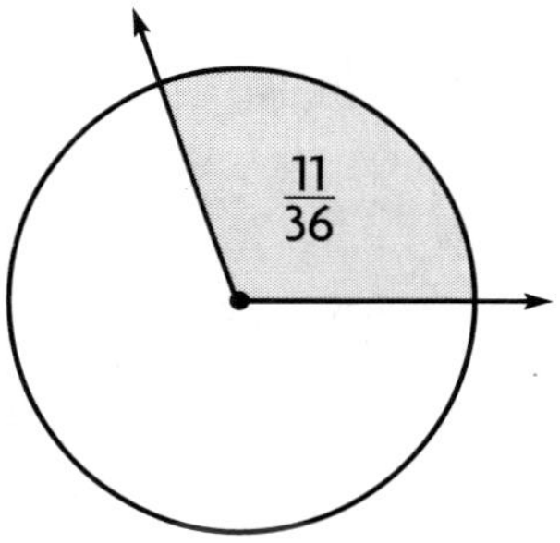

A 250°

B 110°

C 36°

D 11°

21. A flag hangs on a classroom wall. What is the measure of the unknown angle?

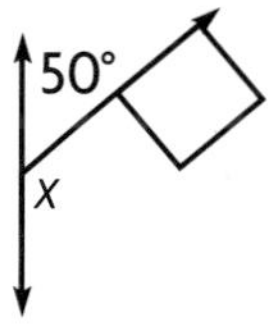

A 30°

B 40°

C 130°

D 150°

GO ON

Name ____________________

Use the figure for 22–23.

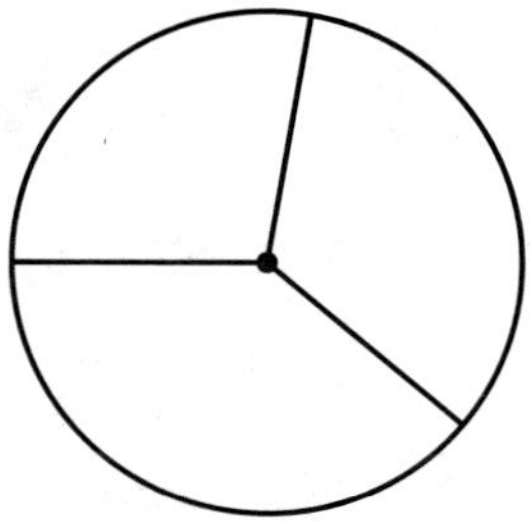

22. Use a protractor. What is the measure of the largest angle in the figure?

A 360°

B 140°

C 120°

D 100°

23. Which equation shows the correct sum of the angle measures in the figure?

A 100° + 120° = 220°

B 100° + 120° + 140° = 360°

C 110° + 120° + 130° = 360°

D 120° + 120° + 120° = 360°

24. Look at the figure. In degrees, what is the angle measure of the shaded part?

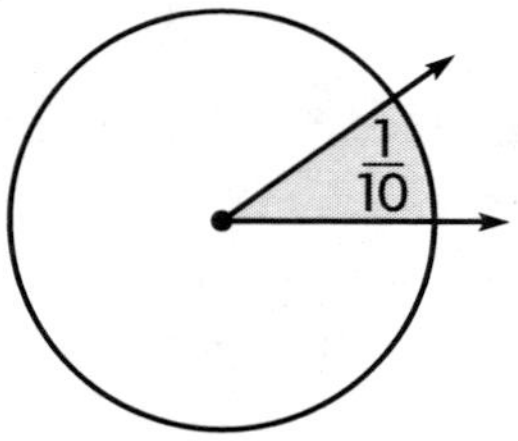

A 10°

B 36°

C 45°

D 350°

25. Use a protractor. What is the measure of the unknown angle?

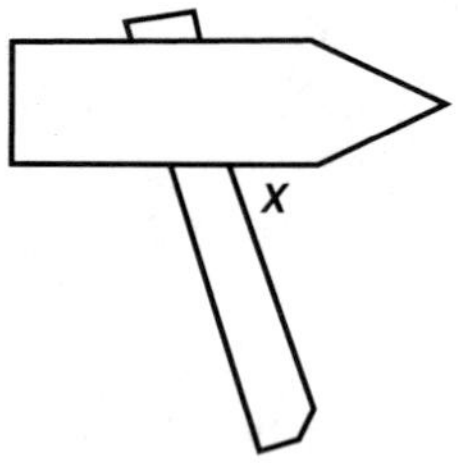

A 125°

B 110°

C 70°

D 55°

GO ON

Name ________________________________

26. What is the angle that represents a $\frac{3}{4}$ turn clockwise on the circle? Draw the angle on the circle below.

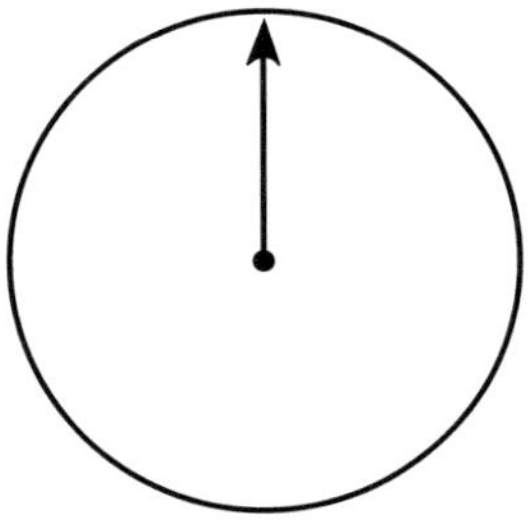

Answer ___ degrees

27. Rachael began walking her dog at 3:00 P.M. She stopped at 3:30 P.M. How many degrees did the minute hand turn during Rachael's walk?

Show your work.

Answer ___ degrees

GO ON

28. Use a protractor to find the measures of the unknown angles *X* and *Y*. What do you notice about the measures of these unknown angles, and is this what you would have expected?

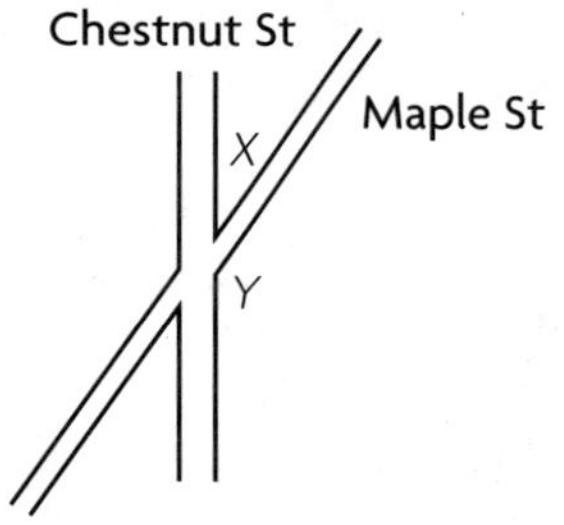

Show your work.

Answer ______

______

29. Jeffrey cuts a rectangle out of a piece of scrap paper as shown. He wants to calculate the angle measure of the piece that is left over.

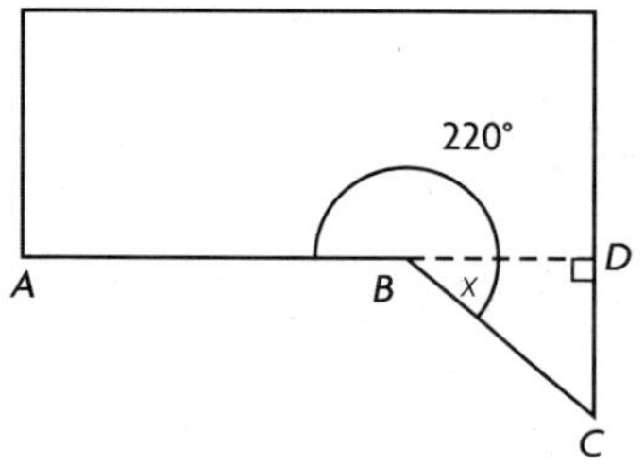

PART A

What is a bar model that represents the problem?

PART B

What is the value of *x*?

Show your work.

Answer ___

STOP

Name ______________________________

Choose the correct answer.

1. Mrs. Lee wants to estimate the height of her garage door. Which is the **best** benchmark for her to use?

   A the width of a paperclip

   B the length of a baseball bat

   C the height of a license plate

   D how far she can walk in 20 minutes

2. Randy is making a fruit punch for the class party. He mixes 4 quarts of different types of fruit juices to make the punch. How much fruit punch does Randy make?

   A 8 cups **C** 6 pints

   B 1 half gallon **D** 1 gallon

3. The Burke family is taking a 3-week vacation to Alaska. How many days will their vacation last?

   A 7 days **C** 21 days

   B 14 days **D** 30 days

4. Kirsten is 5 feet tall. How tall is she in inches?

   A 60 inches **C** 48 inches

   B 50 inches **D** 45 inches

5. The table shows a pattern for some units of measurement. What are the labels for the table?

1	24
2	48
3	72
4	96

   A feet, inches

   B days, hours

   C months, days

   D quarts, ounces

GO ON

6. The tour of the art museum started at 9:35 A.M. It lasted for 1 hour 20 minutes. What time did the tour end?

A 9:55 A.M.

B 10:35 A.M.

C 10:45 A.M.

D 10:55 A.M.

7. An ocean aquarium is home to a gray whale that weighs 35 tons. How many pounds does this gray whale weigh?

A 3,500 pounds

B 7,000 pounds

C 35,000 pounds

D 70,000 pounds

8. Pam saw a koala bear at the zoo. It had a mass of 7,000 grams. How many kilograms is 7,000 grams?

A 7 kilograms

B 70 kilograms

C 700 kilograms

D 7,000 kilograms

9. The table shows a pattern for two metric units.

_______	_______
1	1,000
2	2,000
3	3,000
4	4,000

Which are the **best** labels?

A Centimeters, Meters

B Centimeters, Kilometers

C Kilograms, Grams

D Milliliters, Liters

GO ON

Use the line plot for 10 and 11.

The line plot shows the distance some students jogged.

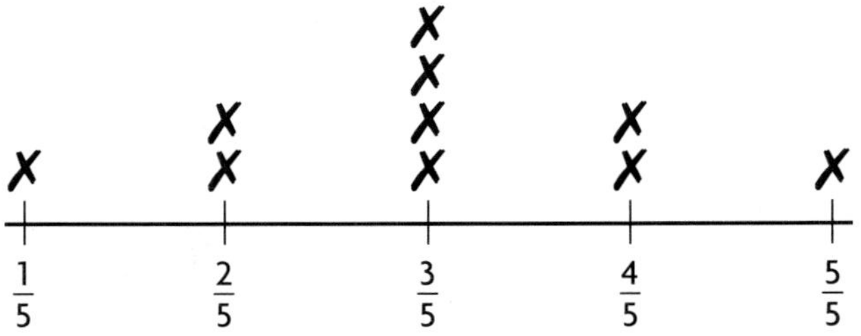

Distance Students Jogged (in miles)

10. How many students jogged $\frac{3}{5}$ mile?

A 4

B 3

C 2

D 1

11. Leah has cheerleading practice each day after school. The data shows the lengths of time Leah had practice for 2 weeks. What is the difference between the longest and shortest time spent at practice?

Time at Cheerleading Practice (in hours)
$\frac{1}{3}, \frac{1}{3}, \frac{2}{3}, \frac{2}{3}, \frac{2}{3},$ $1, 1, 1, \frac{1}{3}, 1$

A 15 minutes

B 25 minutes

C 40 minutes

D 45 minutes

12. Which is the **best** estimate for the liquid volume of a drop of food coloring?

A 1 milliliter

B 1 liter

C 1 gram

D 1 kilogram

13. Which of the following sets of measurements below are equivalent?

A 800 milliliters and 8 liters

B 7 milliliters and 7,000 liters

C 9 grams and 9,000 kilograms

D 5,000 grams and 5 kilograms

GO ON

14. An author signed copies of her newest book for 57 minutes until the bookstore closed at 5:00 P.M. What time did the author begin signing books?

A 4:03 P.M.

B 4:57 P.M.

C 5:03 P.M.

D 5:57 P.M.

15. Mr. Wallis says he is 6 feet 3 inches tall. How tall is he in inches?

A 77 inches

B 75 inches

C 69 inches

D 63 inches

16. Shirlee bought 2 yards of fabric. She will use it to make new pillow covers. How many inches of fabric did Shirlee get?

A 24 inches

B 36 inches

C 48 inches

D 72 inches

17. Ayesha's backpack weighs 9 pounds. How many ounces does her backpack weigh?

A 180 ounces

B 144 ounces

C 90 ounces

D 72 ounces

GO ON

18. Which of the following is **not** equivalent to 200 millimeters?

A $\frac{200}{1,000}$ meter

B 0.200 meter

C 20 centimeters

D 2,000 decimeters

19. Celeste makes 12 pints of lemonade. How many quarts of lemonade does she make?

A 3

B 4

C 6

D 24

20. Kyle is practicing for a 3-mile race. His normal time is 23 minutes 26 seconds. Yesterday it took him only 21 minutes 38 seconds. How much faster was Kyle's time yesterday than his normal time?

A 1 minute 48 seconds

B 2 minutes 12 seconds

C 2 minutes 52 seconds

D 3 minutes 8 seconds

21. Joan is making tomato sauce. She needs 32 ounces of tomatoes. How many pounds of tomatoes does she need to buy?

A 8

B 6

C 4

D 2

GO ON

22. A turkey has a mass of 6 kilograms. A bag of sweet potatoes has a mass of 2 kilograms. How many **more** grams does the turkey weigh than the sweet potatoes?

A 4 grams

B 40 grams

C 400 grams

D 4,000 grams

23. A carton of cider holds 8 cups. How many quarts of cider are in the carton?

A 8 quarts

B 4 quarts

C 2 quarts

D 1 quart

24. Aruna walked 520 meters to her grandmother's house. How many decimeters did she walk to her grandmother's house?

A 5.2 decimeters

B 52 decimeters

C 520 decimeters

D 5,200 decimeters

25. Fred has been taking guitar lessons for 100 weeks. Nancy has been taking guitar lessons for 3 years. Which statement is **true** about Fred and Nancy?

A Fred has been taking lessons for less time than Nancy has.

B Fred has been taking lessons for twice as long as Nancy has.

C Fred has been taking lessons for longer than Nancy has.

D Fred and Nancy have been taking lessons for the same length of time.

GO ON

26. Micki bought 4 gallons of apple cider. Micki says she bought 1 quart of apple cider. Explain Micki's error. What is the correct number of quarts of apple cider?

Show your work.

Answer ______________________________
____
____

27. The table shows the distances some students walked to school. What is the completed line plot that shows the data?

Distance Students Walked to School (in miles)
$\frac{1}{5}$, $\frac{2}{5}$, $\frac{3}{5}$, $\frac{3}{5}$, $\frac{5}{5}$, $\frac{3}{5}$, $\frac{2}{5}$, $\frac{4}{5}$, $\frac{3}{5}$, $\frac{1}{5}$, $\frac{4}{5}$, $\frac{4}{5}$

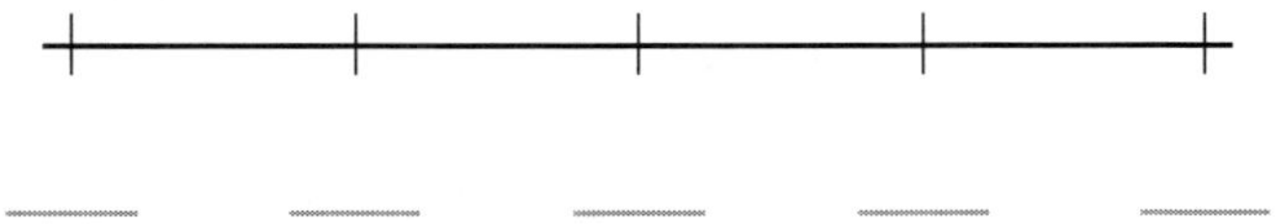

Distance Students Walked to School (in miles)

GO ON

28. Rachel made this table to relate two units of time. Fill in the units in the table. What are the number pairs for the table? Describe the relationship between the numbers in each pair.

Show your work.

______	______
1	52
2	104
3	156
4	208

Answer ______________________

____

____

29. Paul's skateboarding competition will start at 11:30 A.M., but the competitors must arrive at the skate park three-quarters of an hour early to warm up. Paul's round of competition ends at 1:30 P.M.

PART A

Paul says he has to be at the skate park at 9:30 A.M. Is Paul correct? Explain.

Answer ______________________

____

____

PART B

The skate park closes at 6:45 P.M. There is a 15-minute break between each round of competition at the skate park, and each round takes the same amount of time as Paul's round. How many **more** rounds can there be before the skate park closes? Explain.

Answer ______________________

____

____

____

____

____

____

STOP

Choose the correct answer.

1. Kaylon painted a portrait. The height of the portrait measures 14 inches. The width is half as long as the height. What is the area of the portrait?

A 28 square inches

B 42 square inches

C 98 square inches

D 196 square inches

2. Jack plants a vegetable garden. The garden is in the shape of a rectangle. He wants to put fencing around the entire garden.

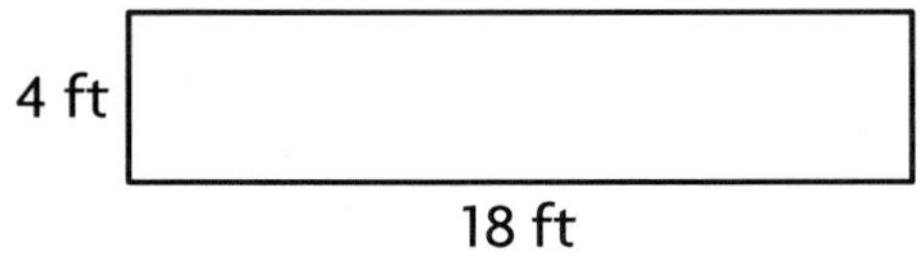

How much fencing does Jack need?

A 72 feet　　**C** 40 feet

B 44 feet　　**D** 22 feet

3. Wilma used 60 centimeters of lace to make a border around a rectangular card. The width of the card is 20 centimeters. What is the length of the card?

A 30 centimeters

B 20 centimeters

C 15 centimeters

D 10 centimeters

4. Lydia cut out her initial from a piece of construction paper.

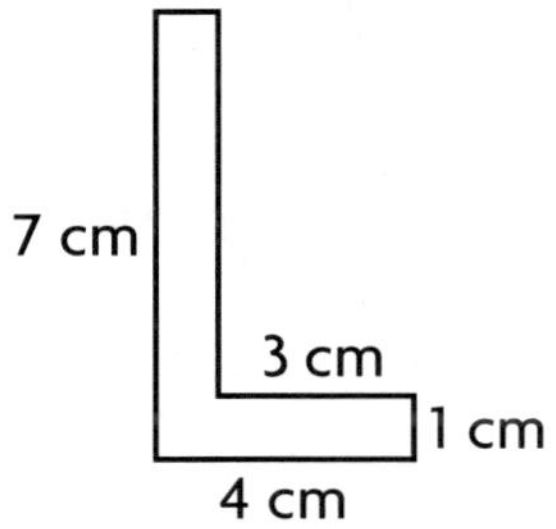

How many square centimeters of construction paper are used to make Lydia's initial?

A 10 square centimeters

B 11 square centimeters

C 15 square centimeters

D 22 square centimeters

5. One wall of Patel's bedroom is 13 feet wide and 8 feet tall. A window on the wall is 3 feet high and 6 feet long. How much wallpaper would Patel need to cover this wall?

A 24 square feet

B 86 square feet

C 104 square feet

D 122 square feet

GO ON

6. Sherry made this arrangement of tiles as part of her art project.

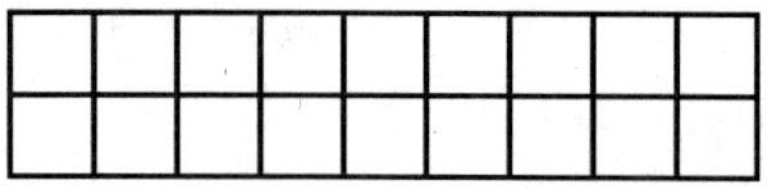

Which of the following is true?

A area = 11 square units

B area = 14 square units

C area = 18 square units

D area = 22 square units

7. A farmer wants to use 200 feet of fencing for a chicken pen. He wants the width of the pen to be 20 feet. What is the length of the pen?

A 10 feet

B 20 feet

C 40 feet

D 80 feet

8. Mindy puts a rectangular poster of her favorite singer on a wall in her bedroom.

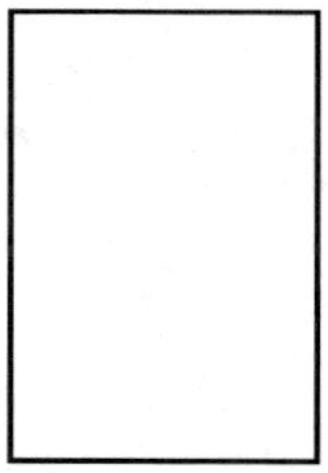

30 in.

20 in.

What is the perimeter of the poster?

A 50 inches

B 70 inches

C 100 inches

D 600 inches

9. Karlie put a rectangular sticker on her notebook. The sticker is 1 inch wide and 3 inches long. What area of the notebook does the sticker cover?

A 1 square inch

B 3 square inches

C 4 square inches

D 8 square inches

GO ON

Name ______________________________

10. A wall is 12 feet long and 8 feet high. Mark hangs a picture that is 2 feet long and 1 foot wide on the wall. How much of the wall is not covered by the picture?

A 2 square feet

B 44 square feet

C 94 square feet

D 96 square feet

11. Mr. Benson built a play area for his children and an office for himself.

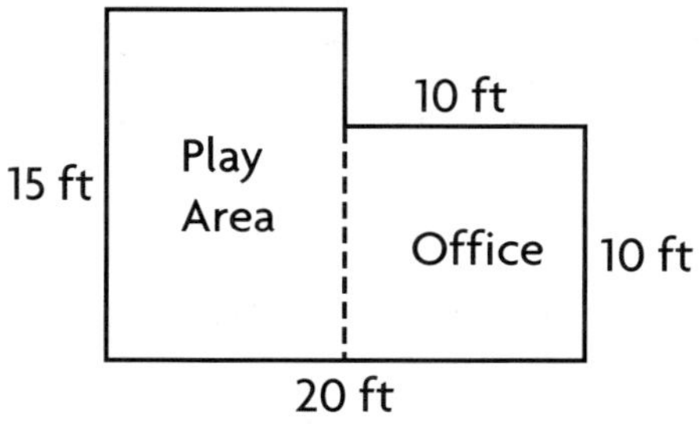

How much carpet does he need to cover the floor in both areas?

A 70 square feet

B 250 square feet

C 300 square feet

D 350 square feet

12. Which rectangle has a perimeter of 20 feet?

A

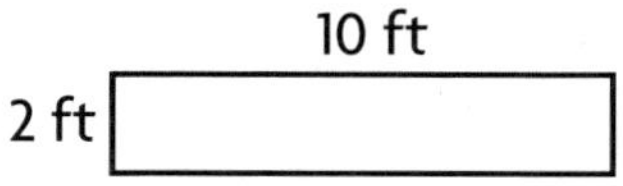

B

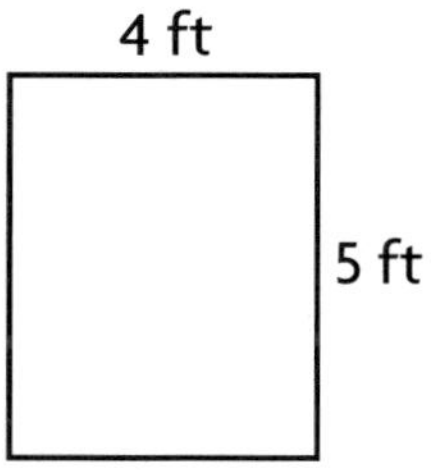

C

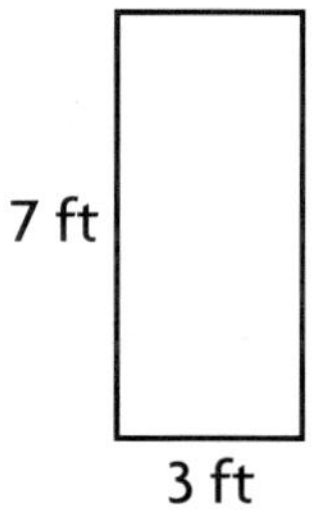

D

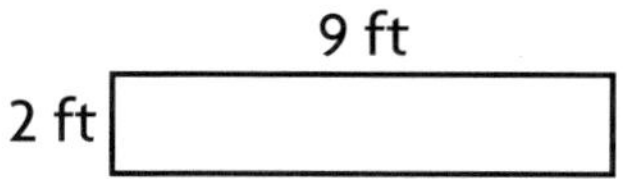

13. Jared is painting a wall in his living room that is 20 feet high and 18 feet long. There are 3 windows on the wall. Each window is 3 feet wide and 4 feet tall. How many square feet will Jared need to paint?

A 360 square feet

B 348 square feet

C 324 square feet

D 318 square feet

GO ON

Name ______________________________

14. A square flower garden in Samantha's backyard has an area of 100 square feet. How much fencing will she need to enclose the flower garden?

A 10 feet

B 25 feet

C 40 feet

D 400 feet

15. The floor plan of the community center is shown below.

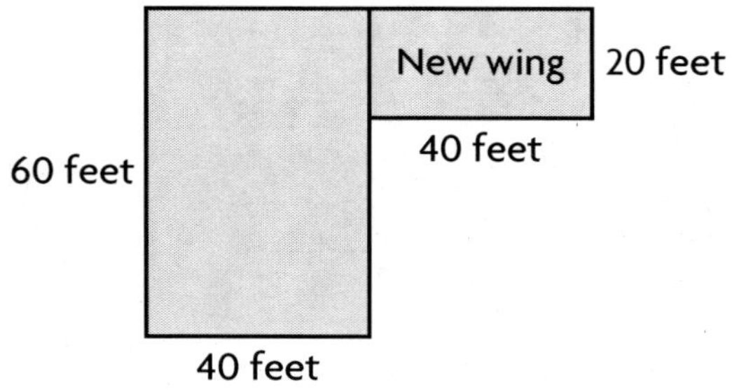

The entire floor of the community center, including the new wing, needs to be tiled. How many square feet of tile is needed?

A 280 square feet

B 800 square feet

C 3,200 square feet

D 4,800 square feet

16. The Wilsons are laying new sod in their backyard. They want to cover the entire yard except for the garden. The diagram shows the backyard and garden.

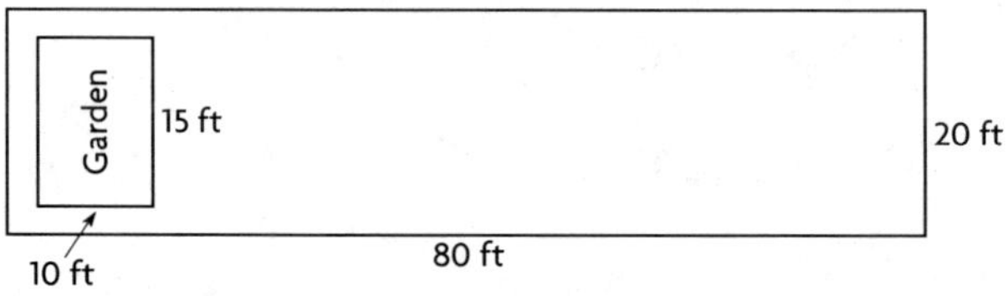

How many square feet of sod do the Wilsons need?

A 150 square feet

B 1,450 square feet

C 1,550 square feet

D 1,600 square feet

17. Laura bought a square canvas to paint a picture of her cat. One side measures 22 centimeters. What is the area of the canvas?

A 44 square centimeters

B 88 square centimeters

C 440 square centimeters

D 484 square centimeters

GO ON

18. Nakela is putting up a fence in her yard to make a dog run. The dog run is 20 feet long and 15 feet wide. How much fencing does she need for the dog run?

A 35 feet

B 55 feet

C 70 feet

D 300 feet

19. The Hernandez family built a backyard patio.

Area = 150 square feet

What could be the dimensions of the patio?

A 100 feet long by 50 feet wide

B 50 feet long by 25 feet wide

C 15 feet long by 10 feet wide

D 10 feet long by 5 feet wide

20. Mrs. Ericson is building a new balcony.

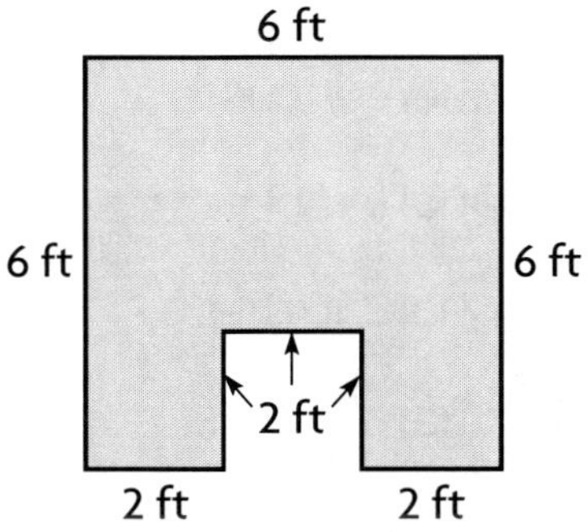

What is the area of Mrs. Ericson's new balcony?

A 28 square feet

B 32 square feet

C 36 square feet

D 44 square feet

21. Aidan bought a frame for a photograph that he took.

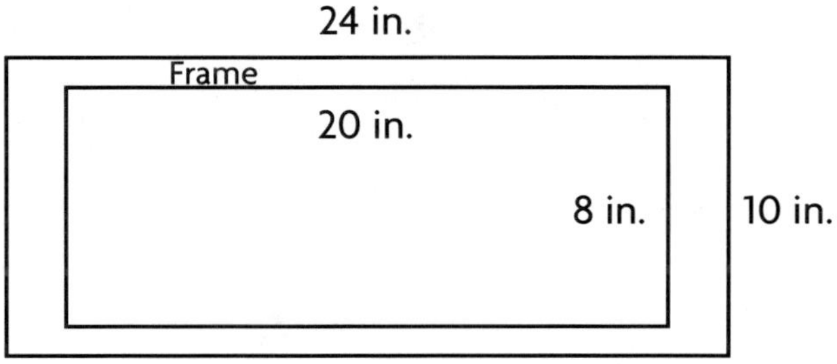

What is the area of the frame not covered by the photograph?

A 80 square inches

B 120 square inches

C 160 square inches

D 240 square inches

GO ON

22. Travis bought a square mirror. One side measures 16 inches. What is the area of the mirror?

A 32 square inches

B 64 square inches

C 128 square inches

D 256 square inches

23. A rectangle has a perimeter of 50 centimeters. If the width of the rectangle is 10 centimeters, what is its length?

A 5 centimeters

B 15 centimeters

C 20 centimeters

D 40 centimeters

24. Workers are fencing off a rectangular construction zone before they begin work. The length of the construction zone is 20 meters. The width of the construction zone is 5 meters **less than** the length. How much fence do the workers need to enclose the construction zone?

A 25 meters

B 50 meters

C 70 meters

D 80 meters

25. Anna is covering the floor of her laundry room with tile.

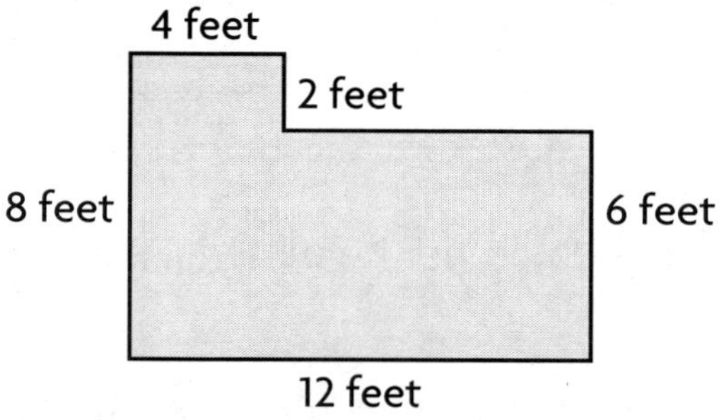

How much tile does Anna need to tile the floor in her laundry room?

A 32 square feet

B 72 square feet

C 80 square feet

D 96 square feet

GO ON

26. Bill drew a rectangle with a perimeter of 16 inches. Then he tried to draw a square with a perimeter of 16 inches. Draw 3 different rectangles that Bill could have drawn. Then draw the square, if possible.

27. The diagram shows the dimensions of Phillip's office.

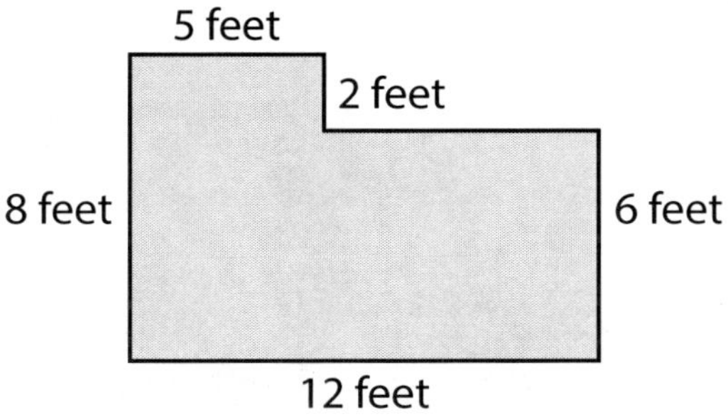

Use either addition or subtraction to find the area of the floor of the office.

Show your work.

Answer ____________

GO ON

Name ______________________________

28. Gretchen and Ed are drawing plans for rectangular play areas. In Gretchen's plan, the play area is 15 feet by 12 feet. In Ed's plan the play area is 14 feet by 14 feet. Whose play area has a **greater** area?

Show your work.

Answer ____

29. Diane made a design using a small square, a medium square, and a large square. She shaded the small square and the outer region.

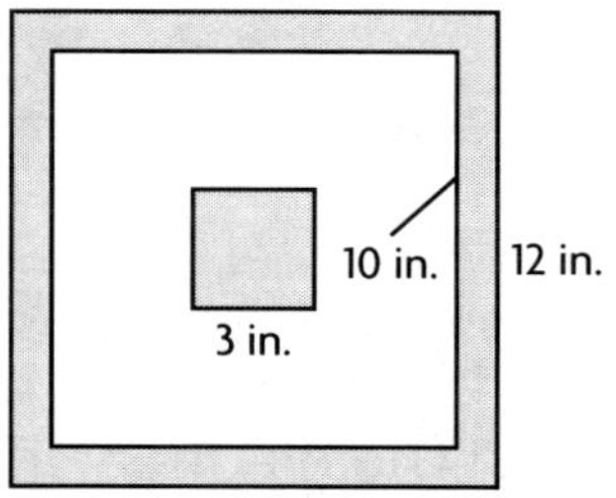

PART A

What is the area of each of the 3 squares she drew?

Show your work.

Answer

large square: _____ square inches
medium square: _____ square inches
small square: _____ square inches

PART B

What is the area that is shaded? Explain how you found your answer.

Show your work.

Answer ___ square inches

STOP

Student's Name ______________________ Date ____________

Prerequisite Skills Inventory

Item	Standard	Content Focus	Personal Math Trainer
1	3.NBT.A.1	Round whole numbers.	3.NBT.A.1
2	3.NBT.A.1	Add rounded numbers to find an estimate.	3.NBT.A.1
3	3.NBT.A.2	Add whole numbers without regrouping.	3.NBT.A.2
4	3.NBT.A.2	Add whole numbers with regrouping.	3.NBT.A.2
5	3.NBT.A.1	Subtract rounded numbers to find an estimate.	3.NBT.A.1
6	3.NBT.A.2	Subtract whole numbers with regrouping.	3.NBT.A.2
7	3.OA.D.8	Solve multi-step word problems using models.	3.OA.D.8
8	3.MD.B.4	Interpret line plots.	3.MD.B.4
9	3.OA.A.1	Find a product using a model.	3.OA.A.1
10	3.OA.B.5	Multiply using the properties of operations.	3.OA.B.5
11	3.OA.A.3	Multiply with a factor of 6.	3.OA.A.3
12	3.OA.D.9	Identify a number pattern.	3.OA.D.9
13	3.OA.D.9	Identify and continue a number pattern.	3.OA.D.9
14	3.OA.A.4	Find a missing factor in a multiplication equation.	3.OA.A.4
15	3.NBT.A.3	Multiply by multiples of 10.	3.NBT.A.3
16	3.OA.C.7	Identify an equation that is part of a set of related facts.	3.OA.C.7
17	3.OA.B.5	Divide whole numbers resulting in a quotient of 1.	3.OA.B.5
18	3.OA.C.7	Divide by 10.	3.OA.C.7
19	3.OA.C.7	Divide by 6.	3.OA.C.7
20	3.OA.C.7	Divide by 8.	3.OA.C.7

Student's Name ______________________ Date ____________

Prerequisite Skills Inventory

Item	Standard	Content Focus	Personal Math Trainer
21	3.OA.C.7	Divide by 8.	3.OA.C.7
22	3.OA.C.7	Divide by 9.	3.OA.C.7
23	3.NF.A.1	Divide a rectangle into two equal parts.	3.NF.A.1
24	3.NF.A.1	Identify the fraction of a model that is shaded.	3.NF.A.1
25	3.NF.A.1	Identify the fraction of a model that is shaded.	3.NF.A.1
26	3.NF.A.3d	Compare fractions with the same denominator.	3.NF.A.3d
27	3.NF.A.3d	Compare fractions with the same numerator.	3.NF.A.3d
28	3.NF.A.3d	Order fractions with the same denominator.	3.NF.A.3d
29	3.NF.A.3b	Use a model to find an equivalent fraction.	3.NF.A.3b
30	3.MD.A.1	Write a time to the closest minute given the position of the hour hand and the minute hand.	3.MD.A.1
31	3.MD.A.1	Determine elapsed time given a start time and end time.	3.MD.A.1
32	3.MD.A.1	Determine an end time given the start time and elapsed time.	3.MD.A.1
33	3.MD.A.2	Determine the relative size of one liter.	3.MD.A.2
34	3.MD.A.2	Select the most appropriate metric unit of mass.	3.MD.A.2
35	3.MD.A.2	Compare masses.	3.MD.A.2
36	3.G.A.1	Classify angles as right angles.	3.G.A.1
37	3.G.A.1	Classify angles as right angles.	3.G.A.1
38	3.G.A.1	Identify parallel lines.	3.G.A.1
39	3.G.A.1	Identify a quadrilateral given a figure.	3.G.A.1
40	3.G.A.1	Identify a quadrilateral given a description of its appearance.	3.G.A.1

Student's Name ______________________ Date ____________

Beginning-of-Year Test/Middle-of-Year Test/End-of-Year Test

Item	Lesson	Standard	Content Focus	Intervene with	Personal Math Trainer
1	2.8	4.NBT.B.5	Use the properties of operations to multiply.	**R**—2.8	4.NBT.5
2	2.9	4.OA.A.3	Solve multistep word problems using whole-number operations.	**R**—2.9	4.OA.3
3	2.4	4.NBT.B.5	Estimate products by rounding.	**R**—2.4	4.NBT.5
4	2.7	4.NBT.B.5	Relate a model showing partial products to a multiplication equation.	**R**—2.7	4.NBT.5
5	9.3	4.NF.C.5	Find equivalent fractions and decimals.	**R**—9.3	4.NF.5
6	9.1	4.NF.C.6	Use decimal notation for fractions with denominators 10 or 100.	**R**—9.1	4.NF.6
7	9.6	4.NF.C.5	Add fractions in tenths to fractions in hundredths.	**R**—9.6	4.NF.5
8	11.4	4.MD.C.7	Determine the measure of an angle separated into parts.	**R**—11.4	4.MD.7
9	11.2	4.MD.C.5a	Classify an angle.	**R**—11.2	4.MD.5a
10	11.5	4.MD.C.7	Use relationships between an angle and its parts to find an unknown.	**R**—11.5	4.MD.7
11	11.4	4.MD.C.7	Determine the measure of an angle separated into parts.	**R**—11.4	4.MD.7
12	7.3	4.NF.B.3d	Add fractions with like denominators.	**R**—7.3	4.NF.3d
13	7.9	4.NF.B.3	Use the properties of addition to add fractions.	**R**—7.9	4.NF.3
14	7.6	4.NF.B.3b	Rename a fraction as a mixed number.	**R**—7.6	4.NF.3b
15	7.8	4.NF.B.3c	Subtract mixed numbers with renaming.	**R**—7.8	4.NF.3c

Key: R—Reteach

Student's Name ______________________ Date ______________

Beginning-of-Year Test/Middle-of-Year Test/End-of-Year Test

Item	Lesson	Standard	Content Focus	Intervene with	Personal Math Trainer
16	5.3	4.OA.B.4	Find common factors to solve a problem.	**R**—5.3	4.OA.4
17	5.4	4.OA.B.4	Find a common multiple to solve a problem.	**R**—5.4	4.OA.4
18	5.5	4.OA.B.4	Identify a prime number.	**R**—5.5	4.OA.4
19	5.6	4.OA.C.5	Interpret patterns with a two-operation rule.	**R**—5.6	4.OA.5
20	12.8	4.MD.A.1	Convert between units of time.	**R**—12.8	4.MD.1
21	12.11	4.MD.A.1	Recognize and apply patterns in related units of measure.	**R**—12.11	4.MD.1
22	12.9	4.MD.A.2	Solve a problem involving elapsed time.	**R**—12.9	4.MD.2
23	12.10	4.MD.A.2	Convert between mixed units of measure.	**R**—12.10	4.MD.2
24	1.1	4.NBT.A.1	Determine the value of a digit.	**R**—1.1	4.NBT.1
25	1.3	4.NBT.A.2	Compare whole numbers.	**R**—1.3	4.NBT.2
26	1.6	4.NBT.B.4	Add multi-digit whole numbers.	**R**—1.6	4.NBT.4
27	1.7	4.NBT.B.4	Subtract multi-digit whole numbers.	**R**—1.7	4.NBT.4
28	13.4	4.MD.A.3	Use a formula to find an unknown measure of a rectangle when given its perimeter.	**R**—13.4	4.MD.3
29	13.1	4.MD.A.3	Find the perimeter of a rectangle.	**R**—13.1	4.MD.3
30	13.3	4.MD.A.3	Find the area of combined rectangles.	**R**—13.3	4.MD.3
31	13.5	4.MD.A.3	Solve a real-world problem involving the area of rectangles.	**R**—13.5	4.MD.3
32	3.2	4.NBT.B.5	Use rounding to estimate a product.	**R**—3.2	4.NBT.5
33	3.1	4.NBT.B.5	Multiply by tens.	**R**—3.1	4.NBT.5

Key: R—Reteach

Student's Name ______________________ Date ____________

Beginning-of-Year Test/Middle-of-Year Test/End-of-Year Test

Item	Lesson	Standard	Content Focus	Intervene with	Personal Math Trainer
34	3.7	4.NBT.B.5	Multiply two 2-digit numbers with regrouping.	**R**—3.7	4.NBT.5
35	3.5	4.NBT.B.5	Multiply two 2-digit numbers with regrouping.	**R**—3.5	4.NBT.5
36	7.6	4.NF.B.3b	Rename a fraction as a mixed number.	**R**—7.6	4.NF.3b
37	8.2	4.NF.B.4b	Identify multiples of a fraction.	**R**—8.2	4.NF.4b
38	8.3	4.NF.B.4b	Multiply a fraction by a whole number.	**R**—8.3	4.NF.4b
39	8.4	4.NF.B.4c	Multiply a mixed number by a whole number.	**R**—8.4	4.NF.4c
40	4.5	4.NBT.B.6	Use compatible numbers and basic facts to estimate a quotient.	**R**—4.5	4.NBT.6
41	4.3	4.OA.A.3	Solve a problem by dividing and interpreting the remainder.	**R**—4.3	4.OA.3
42	4.11	4.NBT.B.6	Divide a multi-digit dividend by a 1-digit divisor.	**R**—4.11	4.NBT.6
43	4.4	4.NBT.B.6	Use place-value relationships and basic facts to divide.	**R**—4.4	4.NBT.6
44	10.6	4.G.A.3	Identify the lines of symmetry for a figure.	**R**—10.6	4.G.3
45	10.1	4.G.A.1	Identify lines, line segments, rays, and angles.	**R**—10.1	4.G.1
46	10.7	4.G.A.2	Use the strategy *act it out* to solve pattern problems.	**R**—10.7	4.G.2
47	10.2	4.G.A.2	Identify triangles.	**R**—10.2	4.G.2
48	6.4	4.NF.A.1	Find a common denominator.	**R**—6.4	4.NF.1
49	6.2	4.NF.A.1	Multiply to find equivalent fractions.	**R**—6.2	4.NF.1
50	6.7	4.NF.A.2	Compare fractions with different denominators.	**R**—6.7	4.NF.2

Key: R—Reteach

Student's Name ____________________ Date ____________

Beginning-of-Year Test/Middle-of-Year Test/End-of-Year Test

Item	Lesson	Standard	Content Focus	Intervene with	Personal Math Trainer
51	3.6	4.NBT.B.5	Multiply 2-digit numbers.	**R**—3.6	4.NBT.5
52	11.3	4.MD.C.6	Use a protractor to measure an angle and to draw an angle with a given measure.	**R**—11.3	4.MD.6
53	9.5	4.OA.A.3	Solve problems by using the strategy *act it out.*	**R**—9.5	4.OA.3
54	6.5	4.NF.B.4	Use the strategy *make a table* to solve problems using equivalent fractions.	**R**—6.5	4.NF.4

Key: R—Reteach

Student's Name ______________________ Date ____________

Chapter 1 Test

Item	Lesson	Standard	Content Focus	Intervene with	Personal Math Trainer
5, 13, 18, 21, 25, 26	1.3	4.NBT.A.2	Compare two multi-digit numbers.	**R**—1.3	4.NBT.2
4, 11, 23, 29	1.1	4.NBT.A.1	Describe whole number place value relationships.	**R**—1.1	4.NBT.1
3, 9, 17, 22	1.4	4.NBT.A.3	Round multi-digit whole numbers.	**R**—1.4	4.NBT.3
2, 10, 20, 28	1.6	4.NBT.B.4	Add multi-digit whole numbers.	**R**—1.6	4.NBT.4
7, 12, 16, 24	1.7	4.NBT.B.4	Subtract multi-digit whole numbers.	**R**—1.7	4.NBT.4
1, 8, 15	1.2	4.NBT.A.2	Read and write multi-digit whole numbers.	**R**—1.2	4.NBT.2
6, 14, 19, 27	1.8	4.NBT.B.4	Solve comparison problems with addition and subtraction.	**R**—1.8	4.NBT.4

Key: R—Reteach

Student's Name ________________________ Date ______________

Chapter 2 Test

Item	Lesson	Standard	Content Focus	Intervene with	Personal Math Trainer
21	2.10	4.NBT.B.5	Multiply 2-digit numbers with regrouping.	**R**—2.10	4.NBT.5
2, 6, 12, 16	2.11	4.NBT.B.5	Multiply 3-digit and 4-digit numbers with regrouping.	**R**—2.11	4.NBT.5
8, 14	2.7	4.NBT.B.5	Multiply using partial products.	**R**—2.7	4.NBT.5
5, 17	2.1	4.OA.A.1	Model multiplicative comparisons.	**R**—2.1	4.OA.1
1, 10, 20, 27	2.8	4.NBT.B.5	Multiply using mental math.	**R**—2.8	4.NBT.5
7, 22	2.3	4.NBT.B.5	Multiply tens, hundreds, and thousands.	**R**—2.3	4.NBT.5
9, 15, 29	2.12	4.OA.A.3	Solve multistep problems using equations.	**R**—2.12	4.OA.3
11, 18, 25	2.6	4.NBT.B.5	Multiply using expanded form.	**R**—2.6	4.NBT.5
4, 24	2.9	4.OA.A.3	Solve multistep multiplication problems.	**R**—2.9	4.OA.3
13, 19	2.4	4.NBT.B.5	Estimate products by rounding.	**R**—2.4	4.NBT.5
3, 23, 28	2.2	4.OA.A.2	Solve multiplicative comparison problems.	**R**—2.2	4.OA.2
26	2.5	4.NBT.B.5	Multiply using the Distributive property.	**R**—2.5	4.NBT.5

Key: R—Reteach

Student's Name ______________________ Date ____________

Chapter 3 Test

Item	Lesson	Standard	Content Focus	Intervene with	Personal Math Trainer
3, 7, 13, 20	3.1	4.NBT.B.5	Use mental math to multiply by tens.	**R**—3.1	4.NBT.5
1, 4, 12, 17, 23, 29	3.2	4.NBT.B.5	Use rounding and compatible numbers to estimate products.	**R**—3.2	4.NBT.5
28	3.3	4.NBT.B.5	Multiply two 2-digit numbers using area models and partial products.	**R**—3.3	4.NBT.5
2, 9, 16, 22	3.4	4.NBT.B.5	Multiply two 2-digit numbers using partial products.	**R**—3.4	4.NBT.5
8, 14, 19, 25	3.5	4.NBT.B.5	Multiply two 2-digit numbers using regrouping.	**R**—3.5	4.NBT.5
6, 10, 15, 21, 26	3.6	4.NBT.B.5	Use strategies based on place value to compute and represent products of two 2-digit numbers in different ways.	**R**—3.6	4.NBT.5
5, 11, 18, 24, 27	3.7	4.OA.A.3	Solve multistep word problems posed with whole numbers and having whole number answers using the four operations.	**R**—3.7	4.OA.3

Key: R—Reteach

Student's Name ______________________ Date ____________

Chapter 4 Test

Item	Lesson	Standard	Content Focus	Intervene with	Personal Math Trainer
1, 12	4.1	4.NBT.B.6	Use multiples to estimate quotients with up to 4-digit dividends and 1-digit divisors.	**R**—4.1	4.NBT.6
19	4.2	4.NBT.B.6	Use models to divide whole numbers that result in remainders.	**R**—4.2	4.NBT.6
4, 17, 23, 26	4.3	4.OA.A.3	Interpret the remainder when solving word problems involving division of two whole numbers.	**R**—4.3	4.OA.3
9, 11, 21	4.4	4.NBT.B.6	Use basic facts and place value to divide tens, hundreds, and thousands by 1-digit divisors.	**R**—4.4	4.NBT.6
2, 25	4.5	4.NBT.B.6	Estimate quotients of two whole numbers using compatible numbers.	**R**—4.5	4.NBT.6
8	4.6	4.NBT.B.6	Use the Distributive Property to find quotients.	**R**—4.6	4.NBT.6
5, 13, 27	4.7	4.NBT.B.6	Divide using repeated subtraction.	**R**—4.7	4.NBT.6
7, 18	4.8	4.NBT.B.6	Divide using partial quotients.	**R**—4.8	4.NBT.6
3, 28	4.9	4.NBT.B.6	Use base-ten blocks to model division with regrouping.	**R**—4.9	4.NBT.6
10, 20	4.10	4.NBT.B.6	Use place value to decide where to place the first digit in a quotient.	**R**—4.10	4.NBT.6
6, 15, 22, 29	4.11	4.NBT.B.6	Divide by 1-digit numbers.	**R**—4.11	4.NBT.6
14, 16, 24	4.12	4.OA.A.2	Solve multistep word problems involving division.	**R**—4.12	4.OA.2

Key: R—Reteach

Student's Name ______________________ Date __________

Chapter 5 Test

Item	Lesson	Standard	Content Focus	Intervene with	Personal Math Trainer
7, 10, 16, 22	5.4	4.OA.B.4	Identify factors and multiples of a number in the range 1–100.	**R**—5.4	4.OA.4
4, 11, 17, 24	5.1	4.OA.B.4	Use models to identify factors of a number.	**R**—5.1	4.OA.4
1, 6, 15, 21	5.2	4.OA.B.4	Use divisibility to decide if one number is a factor of another.	**R**—5.2	4.OA.4
9, 14, 18, 23, 26, 29	5.3	4.OA.B.4	Solve word problems involving common factors.	**R**—5.3	4.OA.4
2, 8, 12, 19, 25, 28	5.6	4.OA.C.5	Use a rule to generate a number pattern or find a certain term in the pattern.	**R**—5.6	4.OA.5
3, 5, 13, 20, 27	5.5	4.OA.B.4	Determine whether a number is prime or composite using its factors.	**R**—5.5	4.OA.4

Key: R—Reteach

Student's Name ______________________ Date ____________

Chapter 6 Test

Item	Lesson	Standard	Content Focus	Intervene with	Personal Math Trainer
26	6.1	4.NF.A.1	Determine whether fractions are equivalent.	**R**—6.1	4.NF.1
15, 17, 19, 27	6.8	4.NF.A.2	Compare and order fractions.	**R**—6.8	4.NF.2
2, 7, 10, 21	6.2	4.NF.A.1	Use multiplication to generate equivalent fractions.	**R**—6.2	4.NF.1
4, 14, 16, 20	6.7	4.NF.A.2	Compare fractions by rewriting them with a common denominator.	**R**—6.7	4.NF.2
1, 6, 18, 24	6.4	4.NF.A.1	Rewrite fractions with a common denominator.	**R**—6.4	4.NF.1
3, 8, 12	6.3	4.NF.A.1	Write fractions in simplest form.	**R**—6.3	4.NF.1
5, 11, 13, 22, 28	6.5	4.NF.A.1	Find equivalent fractions to solve problems.	**R**—6.5	4.NF.1
9, 23, 25, 29	6.6	4.NF.A.2	Compare fractions using benchmarks.	**R**—6.6	4.NF.2

Key: R—Reteach

Student's Name ______________________ Date ____________

Chapter 7 Test

Item	Lesson	Standard	Content Focus	Intervene with	Personal Math Trainer
1, 11, 25, 26	7.3	4.NF.B.3d	Solve word problems involving addition of fractions having like denominators using models.	**R**—7.3	4.NF.3d
9, 15, 23, 28	7.7	4.NF.B.3c	Add and subtract mixed numbers with like denominators.	**R**—7.7	4.NF.3c
6, 20	7.8	4.NF.B.3c	Subtract mixed numbers with renaming.	**R**—7.8	4.NF.3c
3, 14, 19, 29	7.4	4.NF.B.3d	Solve word problems involving subtraction of fractions having like denominators using models.	**R**—7.4	4.NF.3d
4, 12, 18, 21	7.6	4.NF.B.3b	Rename mixed numbers as fractions greater than 1 and rename fractions greater than 1 as mixed numbers.	**R**—7.6	4.NF.3b
2, 10	7.2	4.NF.B.3b	Decompose a fraction into a sum of fractions with the same denominator in more than one way.	**R**—7.2	4.NF.3b
8, 22	7.9	4.NF.B.3c	Use properties of operations to add fractions with like denominators.	**R**—7.9	4.NF.3c
7, 16, 24, 27	7.5	4.NF.B.3d	Solve word problems involving addition and subtraction of fractions having like denominators using equations.	**R**—7.5	4.NF.3d
5, 13, 17	7.10	4.NF.B.3d	Solve multistep word problems involving addition and subtraction of fractions with the same denominator.	**R**—7.10	4.NF.3d

Key: R—Reteach

Student's Name ______________________ Date ____________

Chapter 8 Test

Item	Lesson	Standard	Content Focus	Intervene with	Personal Math Trainer
3, 9, 11, 20, 24, 27	8.1	4.NF.B.4a	Identify multiples of unit fractions.	**R**—8.1	4.NF.4a
5, 7, 15, 21	8.2	4.NF.B.4b	Understand a fraction $\frac{a}{b}$ as a multiple of $\frac{1}{b}$.	**R**—8.2	4.NF.4b
4, 10, 14, 16, 17, 23, 26, 28	8.4	4.NF.B.4c	Multiply a fraction or mixed number by a whole number.	**R**—8.4	4.NF.4c
2, 6, 12, 19, 22, 29	8.5	4.NF.B.4c	Draw a diagram to solve comparison problems with fractions.	**R**—8.5	4.NF.4c
1, 8, 13, 18, 25	8.3	4.NF.B.4b	Use a visual model to multiply a fraction by a whole number.	**R**—8.3	4.NF.4b

Key: R—Reteach

Student's Name ______________________ Date ____________

Chapter 9 Test

Item	Lesson	Standard	Content Focus	Intervene with	Personal Math Trainer
3, 9, 16	9.1	4.NF.C.6	Use decimal notation for fractions with denominators of 10.	**R**—9.1	4.NF.6
2, 10, 20, 22	9.4	4.NF.C.6	Relate fractions, decimals, and money.	**R**—9.4	4.NF.6
1, 12, 15, 25	9.3	4.NF.C.5	Express fractions with denominators of 10 and 100 as equivalent fractions and decimals.	**R**—9.3	4.NF.5
5, 13, 19, 23, 27	9.5	4.MD.A.2	Use the four operations to solve word problems involving money.	**R**—9.5	4.MD.2
4, 8, 17, 26	9.7	4.NF.C.7	Compare decimals amounts.	**R**—9.7	4.NF.7
6, 14, 18, 24	9.2	4.NF.C.6	Use decimal notation for fractions with denominators of 100.	**R**—9.2	4.NF.6
7, 11, 21, 28, 29	9.6	4.NF.C.5	Add two fractions with denominators of 10 and 100.	**R**—9.6	4.NF.5

Key: R—Reteach

Student's Name ______________________ Date ____________

Chapter 10 Test

Item	Lesson	Standard	Content Focus	Intervene with	Personal Math Trainer
6, 9, 12	10.2	4.G.A.2	Classify triangles based on the size of their angles.	**R**—10.2	4.G.2
2, 5, 11, 16, 22	10.1	4.G.A.1	Identify lines, line segments, rays, and angles.	**R**—10.1	4.G.1
10, 14, 23	10.3	4.G.A.1	Identify lines or sides of figures as either parallel or perpendicular.	**R**—10.3	4.G.1
8, 15, 19, 21, 27	10.5	4.G.A.3	Determine whether a given two-dimensional figure has line symmetry.	**R**—10.5	4.G.3
3, 13, 24, 26, 28	10.4	4.G.A.2	Recognize a quadrilateral and classify it into its appropriate subgroups.	**R**—10.4	4.G.2
1, 4, 17, 20	10.6	4.G.A.3	Determine the number of lines of symmetry for a given two-dimensional figure.	**R**—10.6	4.G.3
7, 18, 25, 29	10.7	4.OA.C.5	Analyze a shape pattern to determine a missing term.	**R**—10.7	4.OA.5

Key: R—Reteach

Student's Name ______________________ Date ______________

Chapter 11 Test

Item	Lesson	Standard	Content Focus	Intervene with	Personal Math Trainer
1, 4, 14, 15, 18, 20, 24, 27	11.2	4.MD.C.5a	Relate degrees to angles and fractional parts of a circle.	**R**—11.2	4.MD.5a
3, 11, 13, 16, 23	11.4	4.MD.C.7	Determine the measure of an angle separated into parts.	**R**—11.4	4.MD.7
5, 26	11.1	4.MD.C.5a	Relate angles to fractional parts of a circle.	**R**—11.1	4.MD.5a
6, 9, 12, 17, 21, 29	11.5	4.MD.C.7	Draw diagrams and use equations to find unknown angle measures.	**R**—11.5	4.MD.7
2, 7, 8, 10, 19, 22, 25, 28	11.3	4.MD.C.6	Use a protractor to measure and draw angles.	**R**—11.3	4.MD.6

Key: R—Reteach

Student's Name ______________________ Date ______________

Chapter 12 Test

Item	Lesson	Standard	Content Focus	Intervene with	Personal Math Trainer
1, 12, 28	12.1	4.MD.A.1	Find relative sizes of measurement units within one system of units.	**R**—12.1	4.MD.1
3, 11, 25	12.8	4.MD.A.1	Convert between units of time.	**R**—12.8	4.MD.1
4, 16	12.2	4.MD.A.1	Convert between customary units of length.	**R**—12.2	4.MD.1
2, 19, 23, 26	12.4	4.MD.A.1	Convert between customary units of liquid volume.	**R**—12.4	4.MD.1
10, 27	12.5	4.MD.B.4	Make line plots to display fractional data.	**R**—12.5	4.MD.4
7, 17, 21	12.3	4.MD.A.1	Convert between customary units of weight.	**R**—12.3	4.MD.1
15, 20	12.10	4.MD.A.2	Solve problems involving mixed units of measure.	**R**—12.10	4.MD.2
5, 9	12.11	4.MD.A.1	Record measurement equivalents in a two-column table.	**R**—12.11	4.MD.1
8, 13, 22	12.7	4.MD.A.1	Solve word problems involving conversion of metric units of mass and liquid volume.	**R**—12.7	4.MD.1
18, 24	12.6	4.MD.A.1	Convert between metric units of length.	**R**—12.6	4.MD.1
6, 14, 29	12.9	4.MD.A.2	Solve real-world problems involving elapsed time.	**R**—12.9	4.MD.2

Key: R—Reteach

Student's Name ______________________ Date ____________

Chapter 13 Test

Item	Lesson	Standard	Content Focus	Intervene with	Personal Math Trainer
2, 8, 12, 18, 24, 26	13.1	4.MD.A.3	Apply the perimeter formula for rectangles.	**R**—13.1	4.MD.3
5, 10, 13, 16, 21, 29	13.5	4.MD.A.3	Solve real-world problems involving the areas of rectangles.	**R**—13.5	4.MD.3
1, 6, 9, 17, 22, 28	13.2	4.MD.A.3	Apply the area formula for rectangles.	**R**—13.2	4.MD.3
3, 7, 14, 19, 23	13.4	4.MD.A.3	Find the unknown measure of a rectangle given its area or perimeter.	**R**—13.4	4.MD.3
4, 11, 15, 20, 25, 27	13.3	4.MD.A.3	Find the area of combined rectangles.	**R**—13.3	4.MD.3

Key: R—Reteach

Correlations

Lesson Objectives		Test/Item Numbers
1.1	Model the 10-to-1 relationship among place-value positions in the base-ten number system.	Chapter 1 Test: 4, 11, 23, 29; Beginning/Middle/End-of-Year Test: 24
1.2	Read and write whole numbers in standard form, word form, and expanded form.	Chapter 1 Test: 1, 8, 15
1.3	Compare and order whole numbers based on the values of the digits in each number.	Chapter 1 Test: 5, 13, 18, 21, 25, 26; Beginning/Middle/End-of-Year Test: 25
1.4	Round a whole number to any place.	Chapter 1 Test: 3, 9, 17, 22
1.5	Rename whole numbers by regrouping.	
1.6	Add whole numbers and determine whether solutions to addition problems are reasonable.	Chapter 1 Test: 2, 10, 20, 28; Beginning/Middle/End-of-Year Test: 26
1.7	Subtract whole numbers and determine whether solutions to subtraction problems are reasonable.	Chapter 1 Test: 7, 12, 16, 24; Beginning/Middle/End-of-Year Test: 27
1.8	Use the strategy *draw a diagram* to solve comparison problems with addition and subtraction.	Chapter 1 Test: 6, 14, 19, 27
2.1	Relate multiplication equations and comparison statements.	Chapter 2 Test: 5, 17
2.2	Solve problems involving multiplicative comparison and additive comparison.	Chapter 2 Test: 3, 23, 28
2.3	Multiply tens, hundreds, and thousands by whole numbers through 10.	Chapter 2 Test: 7, 22
2.4	Estimate products by rounding and determine if exact answers to multiplication problems are reasonable.	Chapter 2 Test: 13, 19; Beginning/Middle/End-of-Year Test: 3
2.5	Use the Distributive Property to multiply a 2-digit number by a 1-digit number.	Chapter 2 Test: 26
2.6	Use expanded form to multiply a multidigit number by a 1-digit number.	Chapter 2 Test: 11, 18, 25
2.7	Use place value and partial products to multiply a multidigit number by a 1-digit number.	Chapter 2 Test: 8, 14; Beginning/Middle/End-of-Year Test: 4
2.8	Use mental math and properties to multiply a multidigit number by a 1-digit number.	Chapter 2 Test: 1, 10, 20, 27; Beginning/Middle/End-of-Year Test: 1
2.9	Use the *draw a diagram* strategy to solve multistep problems.	Chapter 2 Test: 4, 24; Beginning/Middle/End-of-Year Test: 2
2.10	Use regrouping to multiply a 2-digit number by a 1-digit number.	Chapter 2 Test: 21
2.11	Use regrouping to multiply a multidigit number by a 1-digit number.	Chapter 2 Test: 2, 6, 12, 16

Lesson Objectives		Test/Item Numbers
2.12	Represent and solve multistep problems using equations.	Chapter 2 Test: 9, 15, 29
3.1	Use place value and multiplication properties to multiply by tens.	Chapter 3 Test: 3, 7, 13, 20; Beginning/Middle/End-of-Year Test: 33
3.2	Estimate products by rounding or by using compatible numbers.	Chapter 3 Test: 1, 4, 12, 17, 23, 29; Beginning/Middle/End-of-Year Test: 32
3.3	Use area models and partial products to multiply 2-digit numbers.	Chapter 3 Test: 28
3.4	Use place value and partial products to multiply 2-digit numbers.	Chapter 3 Test: 2, 9, 16, 22
3.5	Use regrouping to multiply 2-digit numbers.	Chapter 3 Test: 8, 14, 19, 25; Beginning/Middle/End-of-Year Test: 35
3.6	Choose a method to multiply 2-digit numbers.	Chapter 3 Test: 6, 10, 15, 21, 26; Beginning/Middle/End-of-Year Test: 34, 51
3.7	Use the strategy *draw a diagram* to solve multistep multiplication problems.	Chapter 3 Test: 5, 11, 18, 24, 27
4.1	Use multiples to estimate quotients.	Chapter 4 Test: 1, 12
4.2	Use models to divide whole numbers that do not divide evenly.	Chapter 4 Test: 19
4.3	Use remainders to solve division problems.	Chapter 4 Test: 4, 17, 23, 26; Beginning/Middle/End-of-Year Test: 41
4.4	Divide tens, hundreds, and thousands by whole numbers through 10.	Chapter 4 Test: 9, 11, 21; Beginning/Middle/End-of-Year Test: 43
4.5	Use compatible numbers to estimate quotients.	Chapter 4 Test: 2, 25; Beginning/Middle/End-of-Year Test: 40
4.6	Use the Distributive Property to find quotients.	Chapter 4 Test: 8
4.7	Use repeated subtraction and multiples to find quotients.	Chapter 4 Test: 5, 13, 27
4.8	Use partial quotients to divide.	Chapter 4 Test: 7, 18
4.9	Use base-ten blocks to model division with regrouping.	Chapter 4 Test: 3, 28
4.10	Use place value to determine where to place the first digit of a quotient.	Chapter 4 Test: 10, 20
4.11	Divide multidigit numbers by 1-digit divisors.	Chapter 4 Test: 6, 15, 22, 29; Beginning/Middle/End-of-Year Test: 42

Lesson Objectives		Test/Item Numbers
4.12	Solve problems by using the strategy *draw a diagram.*	Chapter 4 Test: 14, 16, 24
5.1	Find all the factors of a number by using models.	Chapter 5 Test: 4, 11, 17, 24
5.2	Determine whether a number is a factor of a given number.	Chapter 5 Test: 1, 6, 15, 21
5.3	Solve problems by using the strategy *make a list.*	Chapter 5 Test: 9, 14, 18, 23, 26, 29; Beginning/Middle/End-of-Year Test: 16
5.4	Understand the relationship between factors and multiples, and determine whether a number is a multiple of a given number.	Chapter 5 Test: 7, 10, 16, 22; Beginning/Middle/End-of-Year Test: 17
5.5	Determine whether a number is prime or composite.	Chapter 5 Test: 3, 5, 13, 20, 27; Beginning/Middle/End-of-Year Test: 18
5.6	Generate a number pattern and describe features of the pattern.	Chapter 5 Test: 2, 8, 12, 19, 25, 28; Beginning/Middle/End-of-Year Test: 19
6.1	Use models to show equivalent fractions.	Chapter 6 Test: 26
6.2	Use multiplication to generate equivalent fractions.	Chapter 6 Test: 2, 7, 10, 21; Beginning/Middle/End-of-Year Test: 49
6.3	Write and identify equivalent fractions in simplest form.	Chapter 6 Test: 3, 8, 12
6.4	Use equivalent fractions to represent a pair of fractions as fractions with a common denominator.	Chapter 6 Test: 1, 6, 18, 24; Beginning/Middle/End-of-Year Test: 48
6.5	Use the strategy *make a table* to solve problems using equivalent fractions.	Chapter 6 Test: 5, 11, 13, 22, 28; Beginning/Middle/End-of-Year Test: 54
6.6	Compare fractions using benchmarks.	Chapter 6 Test: 9, 23, 25, 29
6.7	Compare fractions by first writing them as fractions with a common numerator or a common denominator.	Chapter 6 Test: 4, 14, 16, 20; Beginning/Middle/End-of-Year Test: 50
6.8	Compare and order fractions.	Chapter 6 Test: 15, 17, 19, 27
7.1	Understand that to add or subtract fractions they must refer to parts of the same whole.	
7.2	Decompose a fraction by writing it as a sum of fractions with the same denominators.	Chapter 7 Test: 2, 10
7.3	Use models to represent and find sums involving fractions.	Chapter 7 Test: 1, 11, 25, 26; Beginning/Middle/End-of-Year Test: 12
7.4	Use models to represent and find differences involving fractions.	Chapter 7 Test: 3, 14, 19, 29

Lesson Objectives		Test/Item Numbers
7.5	Solve word problems involving addition and subtraction with fractions.	Chapter 7 Test: 7, 16, 24, 27
7.6	Write fractions greater than 1 as mixed numbers and write mixed numbers as fractions greater than 1.	Chapter 7 Test: 4, 12, 18, 21; Beginning/Middle/End-of-Year Test: 14
7.7	Add and subtract mixed numbers.	Chapter 7 Test: 9, 15, 23, 28
7.8	Rename mixed numbers to subtract.	Chapter 7 Test: 6, 20; Beginning/Middle/End-of-Year Test: 15
7.9	Use the properties of addition to add fractions.	Chapter 7 Test: 8, 22; Beginning/Middle/End-of-Year Test: 13
7.10	Use the strategy *act it out* to solve multistep fraction problems.	Chapter 7 Test: 5, 13, 17
8.1	Write a fraction as a product of a whole number and a unit fraction.	Chapter 8 Test: 3, 9, 11, 20, 24, 27
8.2	Write a product of a whole number and a fraction as a product of a whole number and a unit fraction.	Chapter 8 Test: 5, 7, 15, 21; Beginning/Middle/End-of-Year Test: 37
8.3	Use a model to multiply a fraction by a whole number.	Chapter 8 Test: 1, 8, 13, 18, 25; Beginning/Middle/End-of-Year Test: 38
8.4	Multiply a fraction by a whole number to solve a problem.	Chapter 8 Test: 4, 10, 14, 16, 17, 23, 26, 28; Beginning/Middle/End-of-Year Test: 36, 39
8.5	Use the strategy *draw a diagram* to solve comparison problems with fractions.	Chapter 8 Test: 2, 6, 12, 19, 22, 29
9.1	Record tenths as fractions and as decimals.	Chapter 9 Test: 3, 9, 16; Beginning/Middle/End-of-Year Test: 6
9.2	Record hundredths as fractions and as decimals.	Chapter 9 Test: 6, 14, 18, 24
9.3	Record tenths and hundredths as fractions and decimals.	Chapter 9 Test: 1, 12, 15, 25; Beginning/Middle/End-of-Year Test: 5
9.4	Translate among representations of fractions, decimals, and money.	Chapter 9 Test: 2, 10, 20, 22
9.5	Solve problems by using the strategy *act it out.*	Chapter 9 Test: 5, 13, 19, 23, 27; Beginning/Middle/End-of-Year Test: 53
9.6	Add fractions when the denominators are 10 or 100.	Chapter 9 Test: 7, 11, 21, 28, 29; Beginning/Middle/End-of-Year Test: 7
9.7	Compare decimals to hundredths by reasoning about their size.	Chapter 9 Test: 4, 8, 17, 26
10.1	Identify and draw points, lines, line segments, rays, and angles.	Chapter 10 Test: 2, 5, 11, 16, 22; Beginning/Middle/End-of-Year Test: 45

Lesson Objectives		Test/Item Numbers
10.2	Classify triangles by the size of their angles.	Chapter 10 Test: 6, 9, 12; Beginning/Middle/End-of-Year Test: 47
10.3	Identify and draw parallel lines and perpendicular lines.	Chapter 10 Test: 10, 14, 23
10.4	Sort and classify quadrilaterals.	Chapter 10 Test: 3, 13, 24, 26, 28
10.5	Determine whether a figure has a line of symmetry.	Chapter 10 Test: 8, 15, 19, 21, 27
10.6	Identify and draw lines of symmetry in two-dimensional figures.	Chapter 10 Test: 1, 4, 17, 20; Beginning/Middle/End-of-Year Test: 44
10.7	Use the strategy *act it out* to solve pattern problems.	Chapter 10 Test: 7, 18, 25, 29; Beginning/Middle/End-of-Year Test: 46
11.1	Relate angles and fractional parts of a circle.	Chapter 11 Test: 5, 26
11.2	Relate degrees to fractional parts of a circle by understanding that an angle that measures 1° turns through *n*/360 of a circle.	Chapter 11 Test: 1, 4, 14, 15, 18, 20, 24, 27; Beginning/Middle/End-of-Year Test: 9
11.3	Use a protractor to measure an angle and to draw an angle with a given measure.	Chapter 11 Test: 2, 7, 8, 10, 19, 22, 25, 28; Beginning/Middle/End-of-Year Test: 52
11.4	Determine the measure of an angle separated into parts.	Chapter 11 Test: 3, 11, 13, 16, 23; Beginning/Middle/End-of-Year Test: 8, 11
11.5	Use the strategy *draw a diagram* to solve angle measurement problems.	Chapter 11 Test: 6, 9, 12, 17, 21, 29; Beginning/Middle/End-of-Year Test: 10
12.1	Use benchmarks to understand the relative sizes of measurement units.	Chapter 12 Test: 1, 12, 28
12.2	Use models to compare customary units of length.	Chapter 12 Test: 4, 16
12.3	Use models to compare customary units of weight.	Chapter 12 Test: 7, 17, 21
12.4	Use models to compare customary units of liquid volume.	Chapter 12 Test: 2, 19, 23, 26
12.5	Make and interpret line plots with fractional data.	Chapter 12 Test: 10, 27
12.6	Use models to compare metric units of length.	Chapter 12 Test: 18, 24
12.7	Use models to compare metric units of mass and liquid volume.	Chapter 12 Test: 8, 13, 22

Lesson Objectives		Test/Item Numbers
12.8	Use models to compare units of time.	Chapter 12 Test: 3, 11, 25; Beginning/Middle/End-of-Year Test: 20
12.9	Use the strategy *draw a diagram* to solve elapsed time problems.	Chapter 12 Test: 6, 14, 29; Beginning/Middle/End-of-Year Test: 22
12.10	Solve problems involving mixed measures.	Chapter 12 Test: 15, 20; Beginning/Middle/End-of-Year Test: 23
12.11	Use patterns to write number pairs for measurement units.	Chapter 12 Test: 5, 9; Beginning/Middle/End-of-Year Test: 21
13.1	Use a formula to find the perimeter of a rectangle.	Chapter 13 Test: 2, 8, 12, 18, 24, 26; Beginning/Middle/End-of-Year Test: 29
13.2	Use a formula to find the area of a rectangle.	Chapter 13 Test: 1, 6, 9, 17, 22, 28
13.3	Find the area of combined rectangles.	Chapter 13 Test: 4, 11, 15, 20, 25, 27; Beginning/Middle/End-of-Year Test: 30
13.4	Given perimeter or area, find the unknown measure of a side of a rectangle.	Chapter 13 Test: 3, 7, 14, 19, 23; Beginning/Middle/End-of-Year Test: 28
13.5	Use the strategy *solve a simpler problem* to solve area problems.	Chapter 13 Test: 5, 10, 13, 16, 21, 29; Beginning/Middle/End-of-Year Test: 31